# DON'T LIMIT GOD!
## THE STORY OF GENE LILLY

By Charles  Frances Hunter

published by
**HUNTER BOOKS**
201 McClellan Road
Kingwood, Texas 77339

Ut. #C
46

Scripture quotations are taken from:

The Authorized King James Version (KJV)
The Living Bible, Paraphrased. © 1971 by Tyndale House Publishers, Wheaton, Illinois. All references not specified are from The Living Bible.

ISBN 0-917726-04-9

Dedicated to those people who have never found healing in his wings. May this book give you faith to be healed.

## BOOKS BY CHARLES ♥ FRANCES HUNTER

A CONFESSION A DAY KEEP THE DEVIL AWAY
ANGELS ON ASSIGNMENT
ARE YOU TIRED?
BORN AGAIN! WHAT DO YOU MEAN?
COME ALIVE
DON'T LIMIT GOD
FOLLOW ME
GOD IS FABULOUS
GOD'S ANSWER TO FAT...LOOSE IT!
GOD'S CONDITIONS FOR PROSPERITY
HIS POWER THROUGH YOU
HOT LINE TO HEAVEN
HOW TO HEAL THE SICK
HOW TO MAKE YOUR MARRIAGE EXCITING
IF YOU REALLY LOVE ME...
IMPOSSIBLE MIRACLES
IT'S SO SIMPLE (formerly HANG LOOSE WITH JESUS)
LET'S GO WITNESSING formerly GO, MAN, GO)
MEMORIZING MADE EASY
MY LOVE AFFAIR WITH CHARLES
NUGGETS OF TRUTH
POSSESSING THE MIND OF CHRIST
P.T.L.A. (Praise the Lord, Anyway!)
SIMPLE AS A.B.C.
SINCE JESUS PASSED BY
the fabulous SKINNIE MINNIE RECIPE BOOK
SUPERNATURAL HORIZONS (from Glory to Glory)
THE DEVIL WANTS YOUR MIND
THE TWO SIDES OF A COIN
THIS WAY UP!
WHY SHOULD "I" SPEAK IN TONGUES???

In the event your Christian Bookstore does not have any of the books written by Charles and Frances Hunter or published by Hunter Books, please write for price list and order form from HUNTER BOOKS. For information about Charles' and Frances' video teaching tapes, audio tapes, and price list of Hunter Books, write to: HUNTER BOOKS, 201 McClellan Road, Kingwood, Texas 77339, U.S.A

*ISBN 0-917726-04-9*

Scripture quotations are taken from:
The Authorized King James Version (KJV)
The Living Bible, Paraphrased. © 1971 by Tyndale House Publishers, Wheaton, Illinois. All references not specified are from The Living Bible.

Published by:
**HUNTER BOOKS, 201 McClellan Road, Kingwood, Texas 77339**

# TABLE OF CONTENTS

# INTRODUCTION

During a Miracle Service, as we follow the Holy Spirit, it is difficult for us to focus on any individual because of our attention being on the Holy Spirit. Once in a while, however, God draws our attention to a specific person. At the time of the service, we may not understand the reason, but it usually indicates a special healing in that individual.

Such was our meeting with Gene Lilly. Although he sat toward the back of the Hilton Ballroom, somehow there was a special radiance about him. He seemed to be almost bursting with excitement. We had no idea he was a sick man because of the joy we could see on his face, even though he was quite a distance from us! Sometimes he almost looked like he was laughing as he sat in the aisle seat.

As the crowds press forward at the end of a Miracle Service for individual prayer, we are never aware of any particular individual, as we are listening for the guidance of the Holy Spirit on how to pray for each person.

December 13, 1973 was no exception. We didn't remember any particular person we prayed for and we didn't even recognize Gene to be the same person who had sat far in the back, grinning from ear to ear. The person who got more and more excited as more and more people were healed! The man who should have been worried about having been missed by the healing power of God, and yet he kept rejoicing!

And God was rejoicing, too!

*Charles & Frances*

# BE A MOUNTAIN MOVER

Today is moving day! Get your mountain out in plain view right now, because it's going to be moved!

Have YOU ever limited God?

Have you ever thought, "I KNOW God CAN do it, but I don't think he WILL do it for me?"

This is where so many Christians find themselves, and IT IS TIME THAT WE CHRISTIANS STAND UP AND BELIEVE THAT THE WORD OF GOD IS TRUE!

It's time that we stand up and accept ALL of the fabulous things God has for us.

It's time that we stand up and act upon what God has given us in his word! It's time to "RISE AND BE HEALED!"

*by Frances*

One of the first verses of scripture that I ever came across when I became a Christian was Mark 11:23 and 24 (KJV).

> *"Have faith in God. For verily I say unto you, That whosoever shall say unto this mountain, Be thou removed, and be thou cast into the sea; and shall not doubt in his heart, but shall believe that those things which he saith shall come to pass; he shall have whatsoever he saith. Therefore I say unto you, What things soever ye*

*desire, when ye pray, believe that ye re-*
*ceive THEM, and ye shall have THEM."*

This had the most tremendous effect upon my life because it made me aware of the fact that God was interested not only in the BIG things of life, but he was also very interested in the LITTLE things of life. It also made me aware of the fact that not only did he care about the LITTLE things, he also cared about the BIG things as well. Many times we are willing to ask God for something small but we are afraid to ask him for something BIG.

I wonder what makes us that way?

IS IT OUR FEAR THAT GOD WON'T DO IT?

IS IT OUR FEAR OF WHAT OTHER PEOPLE WILL SAY?

IS IT FEAR THAT WE DON'T HAVE ENOUGH FAITH TO BELIEVE?

IS IT BECAUSE WE DON'T BELIEVE THE WORD OF GOD WITH ALL OUR MINDS, OUR HEARTS, OUR BODIES AND OUR SOULS?

God dealt with me in the area of cigarettes. In my personal life cigarettes were a BIG problem, because I smoked five packages a day, but I thought this was something too LITTLE and inconsequential for God to bother with. There came that time, however, when I realized that in MY life cigarettes were a block between me and God. And so I KNEW I had to do something about it!

As God continued to deal with me, he first began to show me scriptures to prove that I needed to make myself holy and acceptable unto him.

*I beseech you therefore, brethren, by the*
*mercies of God, that ye present your*
*bodies a living sacrifice, holy, acceptable*
*unto God, which is your reasonable ser-*
*vice. And be not conformed to this world:*

*but be ye transformed by the renewing of
your mind, that ye may prove what is that
good, and acceptable, and perfect, will of
God. (Romans 12:1, 2. KJV)*

Then he gave me Mark 11, verses twenty-three and twenty-four to let me know that, if I had enough faith, I could move ANY KIND OF A MOUNTAIN. As a brand new Christian I was really loaded with faith for great BIG things, but it was the LITTLE things that I didn't have faith for. And I sure didn't have faith enough to move a little mountain of cigarettes!

Then God used a pastor in my life in a very fabulous way because he came in to my printing company just as I lit a cigarette. The Spirit of God so convicted me I would have liked to have swallowed the cigarette whole, lit end and all! Instead, I simply said, "I'd get rid of this stinking habit if I could."

He didn't tell me to use my will power, he didn't tell me to discipline myself, he simply looked up, pointed heavenward and said, "Why don't you ask HIM to help you?"

At that point, God put the "mountain" scripture back in my mind.

The Living Bible also beautifully tells it,

*"If you only have faith in God — this is the
absolute truth — you can say to this
Mount of Olives, 'Rise up and fall into
the Mediterranean,' and your command
will be obeyed. All that's required is that
you really believe and have no doubt!
Listen to me! You can pray for ANY-
THING, and IF YOU BELIEVE, YOU
HAVE IT: It's yours! But when you are
praying, first forgive anyone you are holding a grudge against, so that your Father
in heaven will forgive you your sins too."*

God said that I could pray for ANYTHING, and if I BELIEVED, I could have it! The same thing is true in your life! That night I very simply looked up to God and said, "God, I'm a mess, and I can't do it, but if I'm not presenting my body a living sacrifice, holy and acceptable unto you, take away the desire!

At that moment, I had faith to believe that if I needed to move a mountain, if I wanted to move the Rock of Gibraltar into the Mediterranean Sea, it would be done! There was no lack of faith, there was no doubting in my mind whatsoever! I didn't say, "I hope God is going to do it." I stood on the word of God as a believer in Jesus Christ, and God INSTANTLY delivered me that night, and I have never wanted a cigarette from that time on. So strong was my faith in God, and my belief that I had been delivered, that I put a piece of paper in my typewriter, wrote the date on it, placed it on the top of the package of cigarettes I had just opened, sealed it shut with scotch tape, and at 3 A.M. when I finally finished work, I drove by the parsonage and threw the cigarettes onto the porch!

It doesn't make any difference what your mountain is, I believe if you trust God and have faith in the word of God, that mountain has to go!

DON'T LIMIT GOD!

MOVE THAT MOUNTAIN INSTEAD!

Too many times we are afraid something we pray for is *not* going to happen and this is where our faith wavers. Don't let it! Stand firm on the word of God, because God has a lot to say about a wavering faith.

On a trip to Canada, we had a tremendously exciting thing happen. It didn't look like it was going to be too exciting because as we flew in, an unexpected snowstorm came up. The winds were howling and whereas one week before, the temperature had been 93° in Toronto, it was now 28° as we stopped to clear customs on the Canadian side. This was in the spring of the year when all the beautiful fruit trees on the Niagara Peninsula were loaded with blossoms, and pear trees were blooming and beautiful, and all of the vineyards and the other fruit trees were covered with blossoms. It was a beautiful sight to behold, except for one thing. The snow was continuing to swirl and to come down, all the beautiful little blossoms were being covered with white snowflakes, and all of the green branches on the trees were turning white. The economy of the peninsula above Niagara depends largely upon the fruit crop each year. A freeze at this time could have had a devastating effect upon the economy of the entire Niagara Peninsula and many other areas of Canada as well.

The young minister who was driving us to the church where we were going to speak in St. Catharine's was telling us how the people depend upon the fruit crop for their livelihood for the entire year, and so we really began to pray for the fruit trees.

When we got to our motel room, we all felt we were freezing to death because we had not anticipated weather of this kind. We turned on the television to see what the weatherman had to say. It was very interesting, because it was gloom, gloom, gloom, gloom, GLOOM — nothing but GLOOM! All he could talk about was the fact that it was going to freeze that night and they were going to lose their fruit crop.

It's exciting how faith can begin to rise in a believer, and FAITH BEGAN TO RISE IN US! Faith really began to rise in Charles because suddenly we realized what could happen to the livelihood of God's people. We began to realize what could happen to the churches in the area if the entire profit from the fruit crop was wiped out because of an unseasonal snowstorm. We knew something had to be done. We knew something COULD be done! Now, we don't always have this kind of faith. Faith is a gift from God that he gives us at a certain time, and AT THAT POINT we can really connect IF we believe in the word of God, and then ANYTHING CAN HAPPEN!

I believe that God gives us faith ALL the time, but many times we don't recognize it because we do not stand upon the word of God and believe that God is going to follow through on what he tells us.

That night in Canada we prayed and took the authority God gives to believers. WE BELIEVED WHAT THE BIBLE SAYS.

If you only have faith in God — this is the absolute truth — you can say to this Mount of Olives (snowstorm), "STOP!"

You can say to the weather, "Stop!"

You can say, "I COMMAND YOU, WEATHER, DO NOT GO DOWN TO FREEZING!

This is exactly what we did!

We didn't do it in the privacy of our motel room, either, because this would be very easy to do and then come up later and say, "Oh, we prayed for that." No, we did it that night in front of a church packed full of people. We took the authority and spoke just like God's word says. He says, "YOU CAN PRAY FOR ANYTHING, AND IF YOU BELIEVE, YOU HAVE IT: IT'S YOURS!"

He says, "You can say to this Mount of Olives, 'Rise up and fall into the Mediterranean,' and your COMMAND will be obeyed."

Too many times we do not take the authority because we do not believe that we have the right to command something to happen! We forget we are children of God!

That night Charles took the authority of the believer and said, "Weather, I COMMAND you to obey; snow, I COMMAND you to stop; you freezing temperatures, I COMMAND that you rise and that you do not freeze on these trees." Then he said, "God, would you cause a soft gentle rain to fall, a warm rain, to melt off the snow that is on all these blossoms. Thank you, Jesus, thank you,

Jesus, thank you, Jesus." Then we very carefully said, "We'll be so careful to give you ALL the praise, ALL the glory, and ALL the honor because that's where it ALL belongs."

There isn't a thing in the world that we could do to stop a snowstorm!

There isn't a thing in the world that we could do to stop freezing rain!

There isn't a thing in the world that we could do to cause a soft rain to fall — a soft, warm rain to melt the snow away, BUT THE WORD OF GOD IS TRUE!

If you have a mountain in your life, ask God to move it, and believe that he is going to do it, and HE WILL DO IT!

When we came out of the church that night, there was a soft, gentle rain falling. A soft, gentle WARM rain, just like we had asked.

The next day we went through *exactly* the same thing again. The weatherman said it was going to freeze again, but we said, "Thank you, Jesus; thank you, Jesus, we have asked for a mountain to be moved, this time a mountain of snow and ice, and we thank you that there is not going to be any freezing to damage their crop!"

Do you know what happened? The crops were NOT damaged and the fruit trees produced fruit exactly the way God wanted them to.

Is this gift of faith something that just a few people have? No, we don't believe that! We believe that there are TOO MANY OF US WHO LIMIT GOD. We believe that God can do things up to a certain point and then we run into an impossible situation and we think, "Whoops, it's not going to work here!" Beloved, if you have a mountain standing in your pathway, BELIEVE THAT GOD IS GOING TO MOVE THAT MOUNTAIN *RIGHT NOW!*

The thing that I think is so exciting about this particular verse of scripture is the little word that starts it off. In the King James Version it says, "Whosoever." In the Living Bible it says, "If you . . . ." Isn't that a beautiful statement? If YOU! If YOU yourself have faith in God, YOU, anybody, any born-again believer, regardless of how little or how great an opinion you have of yourself, regardless of how unimportant you think you are, YOU can say to this mountain, "Be moved, and be cast into the Mediterranean Sea." Jesus WANTS us to use this mighty power. He gave us authority to do mighty miracles to prove that he is God's Son!

One of the most beautiful and exciting adventures in the world is to stand upon that scripture and believe that God is going to let you move mountains. If you believe the word of God is true, you can say to that mountain, "Go," and IT HAS GOT TO GO!

There are a lot of interesting things to be learned from a story like this. Many times we pray and we THINK we have faith, but because it doesn't happen at that instant, our faith wavers and we go down the drain.

Do you know what the Bible says? James 1:5 says:

*If you want to know what God wants you to do, ask him, and he will gladly tell you, for he is always ready to give a bountiful supply of wisdom to all who ask him; he will not resent it. But when you ask him, be sure that you really expect him to tell you, for a doubtful mind will be as unsettled as a wave of the sea that is driven and tossed by the wind; and every decision you then make will be uncertain, as you turn first this way, and then that. If you don't ask with faith, don't expect the Lord to give you any solid answer.*

God has already given you a "solid answer." God has told you in Mark 11:23 and 24 that if you have faith in God, you, YOU, YOU, YOU can say "Be thou removed, 'Rise and fall into the Mediterranean,' and your command will be obeyed!"

Too many times, after we ask God to move a mountain and we don't see that little inner working occurring inside that mountain, we think, "Well, God didn't answer my prayers." And so our faith begins to waver and it begins to disappear.

When we prayed and asked God to change the weather, our faith could have really wavered the next day when the weatherman said it was going to frost, even though it hadn't frozen the night before. That is the time we lose the victory in Jesus. Because our faith begins to waver, we think, "Oh, he didn't do it; he did cause a little soft, gentle rain to come last night, but look what the weatherman says today, he says it is going to frost and the fruit crop is gone."

That's the time we have to remember what we asked God. If you ask God for something, when he gives you the answer, STAND FIRM! Many times the answer is not in something he speaks into your heart at that particular moment. Many times the answer is in the word of God that you have previously read where he said if you ask and you believe, it IS going to be done! It *IS* going to be done!

Let your faith take hold right then, don't let it begin to waver and don't begin to turn around and look at the circumstances. Peter sank when he did that! What happened to Lot's wife when she turned around to look at the circumstances? That's the time to be strong and to remember DON'T LIMIT GOD!

If his word says he will do it, HE *WILL* DO IT! It's when you let your faith waver that the miracle power of God begins to lessen. Your faith and the word of God are companions.

Don't look at the mountain, LOOK AT JESUS!

Don't look at the circumstances, LOOK UP TO JESUS!

Don't look at the problem, LOOK UP TO JESUS!

Don't look at the situation as it appears right now, LOOK UP AND SEE JESUS!

There are many times when we have a great opportunity to let our faith waver. The devil loves to see that happen! There are many times when you really have to walk on the water. Jesus walked on the water and it really showed something to his disciples, didn't it? Peter, by faith, stepped out of the boat and he began to walk on the water, but what happened? He took his eyes off of Jesus; he put them on the *circumstances* of the waves coming all over the place and he sank!

There are many times as a Christian that we have to walk on the water. I'm talking about walking on spiritual water! Most of us don't have to walk on water these days because we have bridges and we have airplanes to fly over oceans and we have boats that we can get into, so it is not very often that we find it necessary to walk on the water physically, but WE NEED TO WALK ON SPIRITUAL WATER, stepping out by faith and knowing that we are going to be sunk if the arms of Jesus aren't underneath us!

Do you know that some of the most exciting times in your life can come when you walk on the water? When you walk on spiritual water, I guarantee you that you will have a thrill of a lifetime, because this will allow God to do what he wants to do, and there is nothing that turns any of us on any more than seeing God do what he wants to.

During this same time when we were talking about the freeze in Canada, we had another beautiful opportunity to "walk on the water." The pastor's wife had been having a tremendous problem with her back and it was giving her so much pain that she was unable to come to the final service when we were there. A prayer had already been said, but God told Charles to get up and use the authority given him.

Charles obediently got up and spoke to the pain. The pastor's wife wasn't even there; she had to stay home because of the intensity of the pain. Charles got up and said, "I believe God wants us to take authority over this illness, and I'm going to ask you all to believe with me RIGHT NOW!"

He spoke the word of authority to the devil and bound him in accordance with Matthew 12:28-29,

> *"But if I am casting out demons BY THE SPIRIT OF GOD, then the kingdom of God has arrived among you. One cannot rob Satan's kingdom without first binding Satan. Only then can his demons be cast out!"*

This pain was a spirit from Satan's kingdom which he had sent to the pastor's wife. Jesus wrote his instructions very plainly to us. He told us to bind Satan and thereby cut off his power from his spirit helpers. Jesus said that was what we MUST do before we cast out Satan's demons. Charles simply said, "Satan, I bind you in the name of Jesus and by the power of the Spirit of God. I COMMAND you to leave her body right now, in the name of Jesus." Then he said, "Father, I ask you to go back into her body and restore any damage that the pain has done and I thank you in advance!"

HERE'S WHERE WALKING ON SPIRITUAL WATER COMES IN! We could have just let the situation die and left town the next day and never found out what happened to the pastor's wife, but that wouldn't have done anything for anybody's faith, would it? Maybe they would have said, "Well, she got healed in the night sometime." At that particular point, Charles said to the pastor of the church, "Please go call your wife, right now, and we will wait until you come back to tell us what God did."

The pastor immediately got up, went to the telephone and called his wife. She had been lying down sleeping, and when she answered the telephone he said, "Honey, how is your back?"

He didn't tell her that Charles had prayed; he didn't tell her that Charles had spoken the word of authority and that he had believed, without doubting. He merely said, "How's your back?" And she said, "Do you know, there isn't any pain there any more!" The pastor came running back in the church to share with the entire church what had happened because somebody stood on the promise in Mark 11:23 and 24.

You can command it, and it WILL happen!

We had breakfast with the pastor's wife the next morning and her back was absolutely marvelous. Why? Because the word of authority had been spoken with complete faith; no doubting and no wavering. God added faith to his people for a weather miracle by performing a miracle of healing and giving immediate confirmation!

GOD WANTS TO DO IT FOR YOU! Ask him right now!

### DON'T LIMIT GOD!

As we walked into a meeting in Calloway Gardens, Georgia, a prophesy was coming forth. In the prophesy, God said, "Tonight I'm going to do creative miracles; tonight I am going to put things in bodies that have not been in bodies before. Tonight is my night to show my glory through creative miracles."

We really got excited because we knew that God was going to do a tremendous thing. Our spirits had discerned that this message was from God and we knew God was going to do something that we had normally not seen him do in our services. OUR FAITH REALLY IGNITED! All we could think about was what God said, "You can say to this Mount of Olives, 'Rise up and fall into the Mediterranean,' and your command will be obeyed."

In Romans 10:17 we read, "So then faith cometh by hearing, and hearing by the word of God." (KJV) We believed we had heard God speak a fresh promise for that night. THAT WAS ALL WE NEEDED TO HAVE FAITH! God had said he would perform creative miracles THAT NIGHT!

One of the first things that occurred was a man came forward to have a short arm prayed for. We asked him if he had known that his arm was this short, because many people are not aware of the fact that their arm is short. This man was a very tall man and his hands were quite large. I would say they were probably eight or more inches long. The one arm was a whole hand's length shorter than the other. When we asked him if he knew about this, he said, "Yes, when I was very young I almost had my arm cut off and as a result this arm has never properly grown."

OUR FAITH IGNITED! Why? Because we had heard God say he was going to do creative miracles that night and if God says he is going to do something, you can believe that he IS going to do it!

We got excited! We knew, WE KNEW, WE KNEW something BIG was going to happen. Our faith was at top level and we knew that by a command, with the authority that Jesus had given, some creative miracle was going to occur.

We begun to pray. We said, "Thank you Father, thank you Father, we give you all the praise, we give you ALL the glory, in Jesus' name, because we know Father, that not one miracle will happen without your power, and so we ask you, in the name of Jesus, to put the extra bone in this arm that is missing. We ask you, Father, to grow this arm out, in the name of Jesus." Then we began to speak to the arm and said, "GROW, ARM, GROW, in the name of Jesus." In complete view of some 1,300 people, the arm began to grow out! In less than fifteen seconds, God had supernaturally added all the bone needed to make both arms the same length!

We have seen hundreds and probably even thousands of arms grow out because this is one of the very simple things that God is doing today as he visibly demonstrates his power and heals people of back problems. It is impossible to see a back problem healed, but when you see an arm grow out as the back gets adjusted, then it is very easy to believe that the back problem has been healed. However, this was something completely different, because this was not a back problem; this was an arm, the growth of which had been stunted by an accident, so there just wasn't enough bone in it to make it the same length as the other one.

It was really a super-charged moment. IT WAS EXCITING. IT WAS THRILLING! There was no doubt in either of our minds that when we said to the arm, "Grow," that it would grow! The command had to be obeyed because the word of God says if you only have faith in God, NOT FAITH IN YOURSELF — but FAITH IN GOD — and this is the absolute truth — you can say to this Mount of Olives (this arm), grow, and your command will be obeyed. It says, "AND YOUR COMMAND WILL BE OBEYED." It doesn't say maybe, it doesn't say sometimes, it says that your command WILL BE OBEYED!

The thing that we need to remember is that we have to speak with authority and believe, regardless of what the situation is!

We want to tell you something very special. If this man had come to our meeting six months before he did and he came forward when we were asking people who had short arms to come forward, we probably would have said, "Well, that's a different thing, we'll have to pray for you when the meeting is over." BUT THIS NIGHT WAS DIFFERENT! Our faith had ignited for several reasons. We had begun to see God do greater things. We heard God in a previous prophesy say that more people were going to be healed and that we were going to see things that we had never seen in our entire life. Then we heard

God say THAT NIGHT in a prophesy that he was going to do creative miracles THAT night! There was no lack of faith, there was no wavering, there was no wishy-washy-ing back and forth saying, "I wonder if God is going to do it." There was all the faith in the world available if we believed without a doubt, that the arm would grow out that night right in front of everybody, AND IT DID!

Three medical doctors were standing on the stage with us. Three men who, understanding the complexity and the makeup of a body, knew that it had to be a supernatural miracle from God for this arm to grow.

# COME AS A LITTLE CHILD

*by Frances*

Because I was forty-nine when I was saved, there was a lot of speculation as to whether or not it would "last." Sometimes it's hard to convince people instantly that a real transformation has taken place in your life! I had so many questions after transferring from the devil's side to God's side, I almost drove my pastor out of his mind. I called him at all hours of the day and night, because when I wanted an answer to something, it seemed like I couldn't wait a minute, I had to know right then! One time he said to me as I was questioning various things, "Frances, you'll never make it unless you come with the faith of a little child, just believing!" And that's the way I came to Jesus! With the faith of a little child, just believing, and I've never changed. I still have that simple childlike faith I had in the beginning, and I pray that I never lose it! I pray that your faith will be childlike, too!

Matthew 18:2 says:

> *Jesus called a small child over to him and set the little fellow down among them, and said, "Unless you turn to God from your sins and become as little children, you will never get into the Kingdom of Heaven."*

In the sixth chapter of John we find the story of a great multitude of people climbing the hill, looking for Jesus. Jesus knew they were hungry so he asked Philip, "Philip, where can we buy bread to feed all these people?" (vs. 5) He already knew the answer, but he wanted to see what Philip would do. Philip's answer was like most of ours would be, "It would take a fortune to begin to do it!" (vs. 7) instead of looking to God as the source.

Can't you see the little boy with the five barley loaves and a couple of fish? In his excitement, I'm sure he never thought for a moment about whether or not he'd get some back. He gave them to Jesus . . . he gave ALL he had, and expected a MIRACLE! And he received one! And so did all the other people, including the disciples because after everyone was fed, there were still twelve baskets filled with the leftovers!

All God wants from us, is ALL the faith we have, and then he wants us to expect a MIRACLE to happen! If we could just go back to that simple childlike faith and believe that ALL things are possible with God, what a blessing it would be!

I want to share a simple childlike miracle that has happened to all of us who have been born again, and show you some of the biggest faith in the world on the part of EVERY believer.

I'd had a real struggle with God over a simple little matter of sin. I refused to admit that I was a sinner because I had made so many mountains of tuna fish and cream cheese sandwiches, trying to work my way to heaven, but God kept insisting that "All have sinned and come short of the glory of God!" I had a real confrontation with God in a hospital room, but there still had to be forgiveness of my sin, and the cleansing of my life by the blood of Jesus. I argued with God for months, and I honestly believe one of the main reasons was because I didn't really know "how" to be saved. Many churches give an altar call, and an unsaved person only knows that something is drawing him forward, but the part that says "don't do it" makes him hang on the pew in front of him until his finger nails make grooves in the pew! I did that for nine months because I didn't know what to do or what would be expected of me if I went to an altar. The pastor kept inviting people to come forward and "get right with God." A sinner doesn't know how to "get right with God," so I continued to hang onto the pew in front of me for dear life, and each Sunday morning I'd come out of church and say, "I made it again — I didn't go forward!"

Then one day someone put a little booklet into my hands called THE FOUR SPIRITUAL LAWS. I read the book through and when I finished I came to a little prayer at the end and at the top of the book it said, "WHAT TO PRAY AS AN ACT OF RECEIVING CHRIST." I got excited! I couldn't wait to get my kids to bed that night because I knew what I was going to do. I was going to make a secret deal with God, and no one would ever know I hadn't been a Christian.

As soon as they were asleep I jumped in bed with my flashlight and the little booklet, pulled the cover over my head, turned the flashlight on and read the prayer, "Lord Jesus, forgive my sins," but I had to add a little something personal. I said, "But you KNOW I haven't really sinned." I continued the prayer, "I open the door of my life and receive you as my Savior and Lord. Take control of the throne of my life. Make me the kind of person you want me to be. Thank you for coming into my life and for hearing my prayer as you promised."

Instantly I said, "You didn't come in!" (Naturally he didn't come in because I wasn't ready to admit I was a sinner!) I thought a moment, then I said, "Oh, I must have opened the door to my heart the wrong way. I opened it on the left side, and it must open on the right side."

I prayed again. "Lord Jesus, forgive my sins, but you KNOW I haven't really sinned." Then I continued on with the rest of the prayer. I said, "You didn't come in this time either!"

Then I thought, "Maybe it's an overhead door like a garage door." In the security of a blanket over my head, I opened an imaginary door to my heart with an overhead motion, then I prayed again, "Lord Jesus, forgive my sins, but you KNOW I haven't really sinned." I didn't even finish the prayer. I just stopped and said, "You didn't do it!"

I must have prayed that prayer 200 times that night. I prayed it over and over and over and over and I began to think of every kind of a door in the world. I thought of metal doors, glass doors, velvet doors, pearl doors, diamond doors, steel doors, iron doors, aluminum doors, wooden doors, tall doors, short doors, skinny doors, fat doors, you name it, and I thought of it that night, and each time I'd say, "You didn't come in!"

I was frantic when the night was over because I knew I had found an easy secret to becoming a Christian, and yet it didn't work! Nothing happened!

I went to work early the next morning, so I could work hard all day long, just so I could come home and pray again. I prayed the entire next night through AND NOTHING HAPPENED! This went on all week long and by Sunday morning I was a nervous wreck, but a desire had come into my heart that wouldn't be stopped by anything! I made up my mind when I went to church that morning that I wasn't going to leave the church until I knew that I KNEW that I was a child of God!

I don't remember the sermon (if there was one), I don't remember anything, except the song at the end. They sang "Have Thine Own Way, Lord!" The second line says, "Make me and mold me after thy will," and when we got to that point, I thought, "How can God mold me and make me unless he breaks me first?" With my fists clenched behind me, I said "God, break me, BREAK ME DOWN TO ROCK BOTTOM, and then mold me and make me into the kind of a woman you want me to be."

God heard my cry, and God broke me, but do you know how he broke me? He reminded me of sin in my life! Not a big sin, but a little one. I stole a penny from my mother when I was four years old and I never told her about it, and God selected that moment to remind me of it. I was shocked! I said, "God did you know about that?"

Then God reminded me of another sin in my life which wasn't quite so nice. I said, "God, did you know about that, too?" And God said something which has affected my entire life. He said, "I know every stinking thing you've ever done."

That didn't surprise me too much. I knew God could see!

He said, "I know every rotten stinking thing you've ever said."

That didn't surprise me, because I knew God could hear!

Then he said, "I even know every rotten stinking thing you've ever thought!"

Then I knew that HE knew! I cried out, "God, have mercy on me a sinner," because then I KNEW I was a sinner!

Suddenly there was a peace and calm like I had never known, and it wasn't until a couple of days later that I looked down and became aware of the fact that Jesus Christ was actually LIVING IN MY HEART! It had been such a surprise when it happened, that I wasn't even aware of the exact moment, but when I KNEW that I KNEW that I KNEW that Jesus was in my heart, I put my hand over my heart and said, "Jesus, I shut the door to my heart. Don't you ever get out of there." And I meant it.

Now your salvation didn't happen the same way as mine! Each of us is a precious individual in God's sight, and each of us has our own special salvation experience, but this is where the childlike faith comes in!

Can you prove that Jesus is in your heart? I can't! If I died right now, and they did an autopsy on me and cut my heart into little pieces, I doubt if they'd find Jesus there; and yet, BY FAITH, I KNOW THAT I KNOW THAT I KNOW THAT I KNOW that Jesus is living right in my heart.

If you can believe such an impossible situation as to know that Jesus lives in your heart, then you've got all the faith in the world that you'll ever need, because your faith is not in your heart, it's not in any human being, it's just got to be where it ought to be — IN GOD! And if you keep your faith that simple and that childlike it will be the biggest blessing in the world, because if you can believe that, then ALL things are possible with God.

Some people can only generate enough faith to believe in their salvation. That's only the start, and yet that's probably the biggest step in the world! If you've got that much faith, then you've got enough to handle all the problems which can ever come into your life! Hallelujah!

Let's go on from there! Mountains, here we come, because we're not ever going to limit God again!

# "I WANT TO"

### By Frances

If you ever have a day when your faith is "lean," take a look at the eighth chapter of Matthew. This is one of the greatest places I know to strike a match and start a fire where your faith is concerned.

> Large crowds followed Jesus as he came down the hillside. Look! A leper is approaching. He kneels before him, worshiping. "Sir," the leper pleads, "if you want to, you can heal me."
> Jesus touches the man. "I want to," he says; "be healed." And instantly the leprosy disappears! (vss. 1-3)

The faith-building secret of that portion of scripture lies in the words "I WANT TO!" Whenever something comes up and I need a boost in my faith, I read that scripture, because it applies not only to healing, but to every other problem area in my life. Jesus said it, and he didn't flower it up with all kinds of fancy words. He just simply said "I WANT TO!"

When the time came for Joan to go to college, God had spoken to us and said that Joan was to go to Oral

Roberts University. In the beginning, Joan felt God had other ideas, and she visited several campuses, but each time we let her visit, we felt God was telling us "No," because she was to attend Oral Roberts University.

Finally came the summer when the decision HAD to be made because she had graduated from high school. Because she wanted to be obedient to her parents, Joan sent away for the literature.

Normally all universities, especially Oral Roberts, are very prompt in sending the information requested, but the information didn't come, and it didn't come! We waited and waited, and finally Joan wrote the second time for information. This was a year and a half since God had told us that Joan was to go to Oral Roberts University, and it seemed like the devil was going to put all the roadblocks he could find in the way.

It's interesting that God told us to put Joan in Oral Roberts University where the baptism of the Holy Spirit is loudly proclaimed, because this was before we received or even believed in a prayer language; but, nevertheless, we knew that God had said this is where she was to go.

The applications finally arrived from ORU at the end of August. Joan sent in the initial application and then went with us to Washington for a twelve day trip, believing that ORU started on September 28. Imagine our surprise when we discovered while we were on the trip that ORU started August 28, just eight days after we returned home from the State of Washington!

The day we got home, Joanie really got busy and ran around and got all her transcripts mailed to ORU along with a letter from our pastor.

Then we began to WAIT! We called every day and NOTHING had been received. NOTHING! NOTHING! NOTHING! We called every day to receive exactly the same news — NOTHING had been received! We couldn't understand it, knowing the Lord had told us Joan was to be in ORU. Finally they told us they had so many excess applications that we shouldn't have any hope for Joan's acceptance (if her transcript ever did get there!), and said they would probably make a recommendation that she go to a Junior College for another year and then reapply.

We couldn't believe it, because God had been so specific in his telling us that Joan was to go to ORU. Charles "happened" to run into the only ORU alumnus in Houston (at that time) while eating at a cafeteria one day. When he heard about Joan, Wes called several times to see if she had been accepted, and finally the Lord spoke to us through him as he said, "If she was my child, I'd send her up there with her luggage and deliver the transcript in person!"

It was as though God hit all of us on the head. Joan's things had all been packed, the Lord had graciously provided her with a beautiful new Plymouth Satellite Sebring for her very own, and of all things, Charles had a luncheon date that day with the Comptroller of the Junior College where Joan had gone to school the previous year. I called there, asked Charles to bring another transcript home, called the other college here for her other credit, called the pastor to write another letter, and to make a long story short, Joan was on her way to ORU with her transcripts intact within one and a half hours after our phone call.

Do you have any idea how much faith it takes to let your only daughter go off in a car of her own, all by herself, loaded down with all her personal possessions? Do you know what fear can grip the heart of a mother and daddy to send their daughter off on a five hundred mile wild goose chase? It's a good thing we trust the Lord, or we would have never let her go alone. In spite of the tearful goodbyes, there was peace in all of our hearts as we laid hands on her car and asked God's Holy Spirit to just envelop the car and Joan and all who might ever ride in it and always deliver them safely.

She had two days of "sweating it out" at ORU, but somehow we didn't do much "sweating," because we had heard Jesus say "I want to!" We had asked him if he wanted us to send our daughter off all by herself so he could open the doors for a miracle, and we remembered that faith-building answer, "I WANT TO!" We had no doubt that she was going right where God wanted her to go. Even though there might have been a few minutes of human emotion at letting her go into an unknown future, because we knew the one who holds her future had said, "I WANT TO," we had the assurance that everything would turn out all right.

Those three little words "I WANT TO" opened up a whole new world to Joanie. Not only did she have the opportunity to attend Oral Roberts University, but she met Bob Barker, the young man whom God had chosen to be her husband.

"I want to!" Jesus says.

"I WANT to!" Jesus says.

"I WANT TO!" Jesus says.

Jesus WANTS to heal you, Jesus WANTS to help you, Jesus WANTS to deliver you, Jesus WANTS to heal your marriage, Jesus WANTS to make your life complete! Jesus WANTS to give you the job you need! Jesus WANTS to heal your finances!

Ask him right now and see what he says. His word to the leper was, "I WANT TO!" It will be the same for you!

# GENE LILLY'S STORY

# THERE WAS STILL GOD!

All parents want their children to be perfect in every way, mentally and physically. Mine were no exception. My mother gave birth to a perfectly normal baby boy. They enjoyed this boy as his little body began to develop, his coordination began to function, his mind learned first to recognize, then to identify and so soon to be entering his first day at school. They watched with excitement his healthy body and mind respond to learning, playing, doing little chores, making friends and all the other activities which give joy to a family.

It all started on an Indiana farm on November 2, 1939, when I was born.

I loved living in the freedom the farm provided. A farm boy may complain about doing chores or working in the field with his father, but secretly he is proud to be a man, even when he has a long way to grow. I wanted to excel in being a strong worker. I had a desire to be the best in games in school. I suppose everyone is like that.

I had my normal share of childhood sickness — perhaps even more than the average young person. Several times I had pneumonia. In the fourth grade, I had the measles and along with them another bout with pneumonia. I missed almost a half-year of school because of this sick spell, but I was determined to pass my grades with the rest of my classmates.

By taking work home, I managed to pass.

This combination of measles and pneumonia lasted a long time, and along with the sickness I often ran high fevers. At one time my fever was so high that I slept three or four days and nights and almost died. This was during the war years and much of the medication we now enjoy was not available. Due to this extended severe sickness, I suppose, I developed some particular weakness in my body. I was determined to get my health and strength back.

My parents were regular in church attendance and they saw to it that I was right with them. Like most kids, there were times when I didn't want to go, but I'm glad they insisted.

It must have been good for me, because by the time I was eight years old I wanted to be a preacher. In fact, my family often had an extra church service because I got them together and preached to them on Sunday afternoon. I was saved and baptized at a Vacation Bible School when I was about eight.

God saw the warm response in my young heart. Even at this age, I felt a compassion for sick people, sick animals and birds. I didn't know anything about healing, and I didn't understand why I had this feeling. I suppose this compassion never left me. As I got a little older I wanted to be a doctor. Jesus always seemed real to me as Savior, even though I didn't know the Bible well enough to know him as my Healer.

By the time I was fourteen, I was expected to do my full share of farm work. I had been a sickly looking boy since my fourth grade illness. I was still weak, but tried to do my share of shoveling grain, corn, wheat and oats during the harvest. Almost everybody's back gets to hurting and is sore the first day or two of harvesting. Mine did, but they just said, "It's no problem and it will loosen up with a couple hours of work the next day." The pain in my back kept getting worse and worse. Finally I started getting numbness in my legs, particularly my left leg. Then the leg started getting very weak.

The pain in my back became more severe!

They began searching for the cause and I went into numerous hospitals in Indiana and Ohio. My condition continued to get worse. It wasn't long before I found myself down in bed, unable to walk. Both legs were totally numb and I was not able to move them. The numbness soon moved to my left arm and the left side of my body; even my face was numb on the left side. All I could do was to move my right arm and the right side of my face. This all happened in less than six months.

The next move was to the large diagnostic Cleveland Clinic in Cleveland, Ohio. Following extensive tests they diagnosed my illness — — —

### MULTIPLE SCLEROSIS!

They said I was one of the worst cases in the test group. Out of the group of about twenty-five, there was one attractive young secretary, only twenty-six years old, who remained on my mind. Her condition didn't seem very bad at all. Some days she could type, but on other days the numbness prevented it. She was bedfast within two weeks and within two years died.

There was no one in her family who was a Christian. It seemed she didn't have anything to hold on to the way I did.

They thought I might have a brain tumor, so they made tests and took X-rays. The tests were extensive and very dangerous and painful. As I understand it, they injected air up around the brain, expanded the skull and compressed the brain and took an X-ray. By this test, a tumor will appear as a different density. They discovered a large mass of scar tissue on my brain. The procedure caused a tearing and irritation of the scar tissue and left me in a critical condition for about a month. They didn't know whether I would live or die.

The first thing I heard as I regained consciousness was the doctor talking to my mother. He said, "Well, Mrs. Lilly, he will probably never walk again. He will probably not live more than a couple of years."

I was fifteen years old and NOT EXPECTED TO LIVE TO BE EIGHTEEN. That's not a very encouraging feeling!

There is one great advantage, though, in being fifteen at a time like this. You're a "smart aleck!" Nobody can tell you anything. This was a great advantage to me, because I felt I could overcome anything the doctor predicted.

The doctor said something else, too. He said, "If he is healed or if he ever walks again, IT WILL BE AN ACT OF THE LORD."

I didn't know anything about healing, and I sure didn't know anything about the scriptures on healing, but I felt definitely that God would answer my prayers. Yet, I didn't really know how to pray. The only thing I could say was, "Lord, just give me strength. Just help me, Lord. Just give me strength."

People of my church and other friends were praying, "Lord, if it be thy will, heal him." Or, "Lord, make him comfortable." These prayers, though sincere, seemed as ineffective as mine.

For the next eight months they gave me therapy along with other treatments. I improved considerably, but not consistently. As my strength improved, I was taught to walk. My legs were numb, so I could not make them function normally. With the aid of a walker or a cane, as my condition permitted, I would stand, concentrate, and with a command I would think, "Foot, move." Then I would hesitatingly think to the other one, "Foot, move!" To walk a hundred feet might have been a two hour trip at one time in my life, because I learned to walk by "thinking" each step.

Gradually and deliberately my walking improved. There were times I could struggle and walk fairly well, and then multiple sclerosis would defeat my body and put me back into bed, unable to move about. My balance was never good. There were times when a wheelchair was necessary. From the time I was fifteen until I was thirty-four, I never knew what it was to be well.

My hopes for being a doctor were gone.

My dreams of being like everybody else were gone.

I wanted to have a chance to excel like everybody else. This wasn't possible, but I was determined to rise above this handicap. I would overdo the things the doctor said I could do, thinking that because I was young, I could overcome the obstacles. But my body couldn't stand up to the desires of my heart, and I would end up messing up my health again and again, getting clear down, losing, it seemed, all the progress I had made.

I became very despondent at times. I wanted so much to do things and be like everybody else. My pride would be defeated by deep depression.

I wanted to excel, but there was no way I could excel. Sometimes when I would get down, I would reach such lows that I didn't want to come out of my room. I didn't want anyone to see me, not even my own dad, nor sometimes my mother. I didn't want to see my own family because I was ashamed for them to see me on a walker with this infirmity. I didn't want to be a cripple.

I graduated from high school and decided to go to Cleveland, Ohio, to a medical technology school and learn to be a lab technician, because that was the closest thing I could think of that I could do for sick people. I could sit in a laboratory with a microscope and do lab work. I could handle a job like that, because I didn't have to get up and move around.

Again I overdid it while in school and ended up my usual way. I did not know how or subconsciously want, to discipline myself as I should have with the illness. I ended up getting sick again, in fact, I got clear down, probably as bad as I had ever been and had to come back home from school.

I felt very dejected because of the fact that now I couldn't even go to school. I was growing so frustrated, so wrapped up in my own sickness sometimes, that I felt I was losing the compassion I always had for others. I was becoming hardened, yet under this hard exterior crust there remained a flicker of compassion for sick and afflicted people. In spite of myself, THERE WAS STILL GOD!

# HER NAME WAS PHYLLIS!

A pretty girl named Phyllis moved to Hagerstown when we were in the eighth grade. While we attended school together, we didn't start dating until after high school. But I always had my eye on this five-foot four-inch beauty.

The first time I took her out on a date I had the nerve to tell her I wanted to marry her.

Phyllis, unfortunately, at the time, didn't exactly share that dream. She has often said she thought I was an awfully "scrawny-looking kid" and wished I'd go away and leave her alone! That's not exactly what you call admiration.

While I classified myself as the self-appointed president of her admiration society, she held me at arm's length. I really thought it was a big deal when she consented to go with me to a drive-in for a coke.

But I had some nerve! Imagine, asking such a neat gal out when I was a multiple sclerosis victim. I must confess I was also selfish.

I'm not certain what tipped the scale in my favor, or when exactly Phyllis started regarding me as somebody other than a skinny nuisance. But she did! PRAISE GOD SHE DID!

Together we started dreaming. It all happened rather suddenly the summer after graduation from high school. I knew without a shadow of a doubt that she was the girl I wanted to spend the rest of my life with.

Even though I was in this condition — and Phyllis knew it — still she loved me. She wanted for us to be married.

Now she admits that she didn't know all the ramifications of the disease multiple sclerosis, but even had she known, she insists that her love was such that she wouldn't have thrown me overboard. It wasn't that she wasn't warned; she was. My mother saw to that because, in all fairness, she felt this young girl needed to know what the consequences of the disease might be in later years.

Not only did Mother attempt to discourage Phyllis from marrying me because of the multiple sclerosis, she considered that we were about to be unequally yoked.

Phyllis had not been raised in a church-going family. She knew nothing about God. About the only reference she'd ever heard to God was my statement that I prayed to the Lord to give me strength when I'd been told some years before that I had multiple sclerosis. I told her I guessed that God heard my prayer because I sure wasn't down in bed now.

When I went to Cleveland I left her behind. Mother helped me pack my belongings, but the one thing — person, really — that I wanted to take with me had to remain in Hagerstown. Later when I had to give up my dream of becoming a lab technician, I did not give up my dream of the one remaining bright spot in my life — Phyllis!

My faith was mighty flimsy for a guy who'd been going to church all his life, and who was supposed to have invited Jesus into his heart at the age of about eight.

I wasn't adverse either to pressing my advantage at this point, and letting Phyllis think that God had smiled on me and things weren't really going to be all that bad. Who knows? Maybe I'll even outgrow this thing. I didn't say it to her, but I rather imagine by other things I said that I led her along to believe that my mother's warnings were a bit exaggerated. You'd better believe I didn't want to let this girl slip away from me.

Little did either of us know about God's plan for our lives. Little did we know of his patience and love.

And little did we know what awaited us in the next ten years! Had either of us had any inkling of what lay ahead, I'm sure, on my part, I'd have selfishly hung in there ready and willing to drag Phyllis down the tortuous path with me; but Phyllis, because she is a woman with great common sense, might have thought twice and insisted that we receive counsel and help before things got so out-of-hand.

I wonder if there are special rewards in heaven for women like my Phyllis. My dreams were all wrapped up in her.

Before I returned home from school while I was still eighteen, Phyllis and I made plans to get married, even in my condition. Although Phyllis was not raised in church and did not know the Lord, she went to church with me many times. Then she started going regularly with me. We went to a little Friends Church. One time we went to Indianapolis, Indiana, to a Billy Graham Crusade and there Phyllis received Jesus as her Savior.

One time shortly before we got married, we were out riding around with some friends on a Sunday afternoon. My leg muscles suddenly started drawing. Spasms such as this are not uncommon with multiple sclerosis, but the seizure that day drew me up into a ball.

The spasms kept getting worse and worse, and I was getting weaker and weaker. Finally it was so bad that I couldn't even control my movements any more. I was scared! They took me to a hospital and I was totally out like I was under an anesthetic. The doctors feared that my joints would actually be pulled out of their sockets.

Anesthesia was given and mercifully I lay for days unaware of what was going on about me.

To my parents the doctors indicated that brain surgery might be necessary. It would have, of course, been very dangerous surgery — not only dangerous, but I could have died — or if the surgery had not been altogether successful I could have been paralyzed for the rest of my life. But the spasms stopped and they decided not to have surgery.

Recovery was painfully slow but eventually I was back on my feet. Then my dream came true when our marriage took place! Phyllis was uncommonly brave throughout the entire ordeal and I was the happiest I had ever been.

I was able to work at a hospital in New Castle, Indiana for a short time after we were married. But the pace of working was too much for my body, and I had to quit. I tried going back to school and found I couldn't do that either. I needed rest, lots of rest. When I tried to carry a load or responsibility, I couldn't handle it.

What was I to do? The exertion required for work or studies was too much of a drain and I'd constantly lose the battle physically. Now I was a married man. More than ever I felt the compulsion to make something of my life.

As I struggled with the realization that multiple sclerosis imposed limiting factors on my future, I found satisfaction in becoming involved with a youth group at the church we were attending. This was something Phyllis and I enjoyed doing together. It was a growing group. We kept everyone busy and coming back for more activities.

Phyllis was working and contributing to our support. We had decided that we wanted a family. I was twenty and although the future looked uncertain, still there was a determination that kept me going. And then Phyllis had our first child, Doug.

A medical missionary from Kenya, Africa was home on furlough and, as I listened to him speak, my heart was challenged. There was the old familiar stirring — medicine — becoming a doctor, the dream I'd abandoned earlier at the outset of my battle with multiple sclerosis. Could it possibly be? Could we go to the mission field?

Phyllis was very concerned about this dream I was nurturing. She was also very aware of our need for security, and the whole idea was frustrating to her. In spite of all this, she was still willing to go but was not excited about it like I was. Nevertheless, we were making plans to go. The missionary was helping us. Plans had progressed to the extent that he was instructing us in packing for overseas.

Then someone said to us, "You can't go to the mission field. If you do, we'll never be able to get medicine to you and you'll probably die."

That scared me so much that we decided they were probably right, so we abandoned our plans. It disturbed me because I wasn't sure how God felt about our decision. I wanted to do what he wanted, but I wasn't sure of his plans.

When we didn't go to the mission field, it seemed that our family took a turn for the worse. It was as though the devil put a ring in my nose and started leading me around. The thing that became very important in my life was money. I knew we had to have money for our family. By this time, our second child Gina, had been born. I lived with panic for a time but determined that I would provide for my family.

It is interesting that during that time, as I look back on it, no one ever encouraged us to go into the ministry. When I talked about the ministry it seemed people expected you to hear thunder crashing and see lightning flashing — you had to have something dramatic happen if God was speaking to you. Obviously, since I wasn't hearing thunder or seeing lightning or hearing God's voice from a burning bush, everyone felt this was just another of my foolish dreams. They suggested we pray about it again. But when I started out to make money with such a determination that I would give up everything to do it, everyone encouraged me. When I talked of going into business for myself, suddenly everybody was gathering around, slapping me on the back and saying, "Boy, that's great. I hope you have tremendous success."

An uncontrollable fear began to possess me. Fear that I wouldn't be able to care for my family physically or financially. Fear of what people would think if I failed. Fear bred greed and a driving lust to make money came upon me. I wanted to make all the money I possibly could and I was willing to give up everything to do it.

I didn't know much about the furniture business but I decided that would be my way to success. On my twenty-first birthday we opened our furniture store. Even with very little money, we managed to acquire a lot of inventory. But in a small town we couldn't sell enough and soon went broke and had to close the store.

This was a very frustrating experience. I was discouraged and embarrassed. I got depressed. People would try to help by assuring me I could have made it go if I had been in good health. I felt this way too, but it still hurt inside. It also provided an excellent excuse.

No longer were we active in church. I was devoting every ounce of energy I possessed to making money since I wouldn't likely be able to work and live a normal life and probably wouldn't live to be very old. Phyllis and the kids had to be taken care of now.

A hardness settled in my heart because the Lord was not in the center of our lives. In just a very short while our marriage started going on the rocks. Our love for each other grew colder. Before long I started doing things I shouldn't do.

Even though I was on my walker or using a cane or stick, I got to running around with the wrong crowd. I would go to taverns and carry on and drink. This made it even harder on my health.

I'd always been interested in cars, even as a young boy. The thrill of a fast ride in an automobile was something I liked. The idea came to me, "Why not drive a race car?" Why not! That would be an easy way for me to do one of two things — get killed or get rich!

As I look back now, had I been honest with myself, I believe that the real motive in my wanting to drive race cars was nothing but a spirit of suicide. I was just trying to get away from it all, trying to kill myself. I think this was the real reason for drinking and not getting the proper rest. Our marriage had reached the point that it was a total wreck, and I wanted to die.

I reasoned that Phyllis was a capable woman and could carry on even better without me. With me and the hospital bills and doctor bills out of the way, she could do very well. It just seemed like the best thing in the world was for me to die and let Phyllis and the children go on.

Another thing, in all honesty, I HAD A FEAR OF GETTING WELL. Then I would have no excuse for failure.

Satan is really a deceiver. He very cleverly, slowly, and systematically began replacing my desire to please God and my family with a deceitful desire to please self. When self couldn't be pleased, self-pity became my ruler. He created a lie in my mind to cause me to believe self-destruction would bring satisfaction. He hid from my mind the truth that God commands us NOT to murder. I even believed that if I died by a self-inflicted "accident" or if I caused my poor health to bring on my death, God really wouldn't know, and I could still go to heaven. Or, had I given up hope for this life as well as for eternity? Satan tried hard to rush my end and put me into an eternal hell of terror and torture. But God in his patient mercy and love still wanted me. He never gives up, even if we do.

# SUCCESS???

I HAD TO GO ON. I tried to sell, but nothing worked. I landed a job in a factory as a lab metallurgist. That lasted until the group insurance became a factor, forcing me out.

I had become a very resentful person because of my sickness and defeat. About the only thing Phyllis and I had in common by this time was a mail box. We had spent ten years that really weren't a marriage. I had done about everything wrong that a man could do to his family. I failed to provide for them. I went all over the country driving race cars. I ran around on my wife. I had totally fallen away from God.

I tried my hand at data processing and that ended with a parting of the ways.

Then a man came along and offered me what I felt was a way to finally make real good money. And he talked about the Lord! I thought, "This will really be an opportunity for me!" I managed to scrape together some money, bought into a company which sold franchises and operated a retail business.

Not long after we started with this company, they lost their legal right to operate in Indiana. We transferred to Phoenix, Arizona. We had begun to make money, but we spent it all and when we arrived in Phoenix, we were broke again. We didn't even own a car.

In our search for the answer to life and success in business, we got involved in a lot of mind-control courses. Think and grow rich! We studied all kinds of positive thinking courses. We got involved in occults. We studied astrology, ESP and practically every cult that came our way. Satan had set new traps to capture us. The leaders of the company talked about God, but actually were responsible for a lot of this devilish teaching we were drawn into. They talked about the Bible, but they didn't know Jesus. Satan talks about God and the Bible, but he was defeated by Jesus. Any time we turn away from Jesus, Satan is ready to trick us to follow him.

Away from all home-town influences — from family and friends who knew us — Phyllis and I found ourselves working to put our relationship into a better condition. We came to the point where we recognized that we were either going to try to make a go of our marriage or we'd best get a divorce. I was willing to make any change in my life to allow us to continue living together and have our home. I know now that a home without Jesus is no more than a house. Phyllis and I began to depend more and more on one another, because we were working together in this business.

My up and down life of being sick and partially well continued.

The business had a certain amount of success, but not much. We began getting salespeople to work for us. One day at home a new breadman came to deliver our fresh bread. As we met him at the door, he was a bundle of enthusiasm and filled with excitement. I knew immediately that I needed him to work for me as a salesman. I asked him to come in and said, "You're a pretty good breadman. What are you doing delivering bread?"

His reply wasn't what I'd expected! "Well, I'm out here to start a new church. I have two other couples here to start a United Brethren Church. It's a mission work, so I deliver bread to make a living." He then said, "Of course, we minister as we are building the church. I'd like to invite you to come."

I said, "I'd like to put you to work in my business!" He didn't accept my offer, but did keep coming by our house to hold a Bible study just for us. We understood so very little about the Lord and he really affected our lives by teaching us.

I had been rebellious about going to church because I didn't believe in what I saw in churches. I saw the hypocrites at church on Sunday morning that I met at the bar Saturday night. I didn't think about the fact that they were saying the same thing about me. I'm glad I have learned since then not to let a hyprocrite send me to hell. I've learned to look at Jesus instead of people.

I had become so hardened to the gospel, the people, the church and to life that I became seared to the whole truth of life and the real desires in my life. The "get-rich-company" demanded much of my time. They said we could help others as we made our money, and that sounded good. But we really didn't help others — we just "used" them. I didn't realize I had become blind to what was actually taking place.

But this minister breadman kept seeing us and teaching the Bible to us until we found ourselves in church again. We began to have a renewed desire to serve the Lord.

The devil knew about this and worked his way back in through a promotion we received in the company. We were removed from the distributor list and began training other people to become like *we were*. As I look back today, this is a frightening thought because we were a mess.

They sent us to Reno, Nevada for school and then we came back to Phoenix. Once more, we got too busy to think of the Lord and started falling away again.

Then we moved to Dallas, Texas. We were kept busy on Sundays with sales meetings and other activities and had no time for church. It didn't seem important, anyway.

Phyllis and I grew closer together, really for the sake of making money, but in the process we forgot our children, Doug and Gina. We didn't provide the right kind of home for them nor give them the attention they needed. They had never known me to be well, and seeing me sick all the time was hard on them. There was a lot of fear and frustration in our home.

I was on an ego trip!

The company called it motivation.

They called it promotions and I received one right after another. By whatever name you choose to call it, it never satisfies. Only Jesus can satisfy and he alone is a safe motivation. But my mind had no time for him — the promotions were more real to me. Positive thinking, self-hypnosis — they taught me that the answer to success was in your mind.

I was enjoying the best period of health that I'd had since early childhood. I still had health problems and often had to get up two hours early to get my legs to functioning, but I was going strong. We were moved again, this time to Reno. Things were going great! I was traveling a lot and by now we were flying. It seemed like the money would never end. We were buying diamond rings and had a Cadillac and nice clothes. Boy, everything was "hunky-dory," just what we had always looked for. Just what we always wanted. I was still drinking some and smoking and doing things which were not good for my body. Nothing really satisfies when it's done to please self.

In our search for the always evasive satisfaction, we began to gamble for fun. But, it wasn't long until the fun became serious and we were gambling more than we ought to. When a person lives this kind of life, it's a never-ending race to satisfy. It's a very poor kind of life. When I got home at night, it was all I could do to literally collapse in bed. If I could find the energy and strength, I would get up and we would go downtown to gamble or drink or go to a show or do something to fill up the void we were experiencing in our lives.

Vicki was our friend and secretary. She didn't know the Lord, and had recently been divorced. She was excited about falling into this motivation thing. But Vicki started going to church. Another girl at the warehouse had invited her to church. When I was out of town, sometimes she'd take Phyllis. Vicki and Phyllis didn't really know what to think about the church. People would clap their hands and praise the Lord and they just sensed that the presence of the Lord was there. Phyllis would try to get me to go; but I "never had the strength." She'd take the kids once in a while. I was no encouragement to her whatsoever. I ONLY HAD THE STRENGTH TO DO WHAT *I* WANTED TO DO!

Phyllis was finally really getting ahold of God. Do you know what happened in our company as soon as she really got hold of God and wanted to go to church? We got moved from Reno back to Dallas!

EVERY TIME WE STARTED TO GET CLOSE TO JESUS, WE GOT A PROMOTION! All these promotions were so well-timed, because they always seemed to come just as we got interested in God.

We came back to Dallas with great expectations of getting richer and living in the fine part of the city, driving a Cadillac, and having all the things anyone could want. But we didn't have Jesus, and I was getting more and more sick. I knew that for the last year and a half my health had really been going down.

Dallas, too, was short-lived.

From Dallas we were moved to Montgomery, Alabama. In Montgomery we met with what most people would call success.

We had a good income!

We lived in a townhouse across the pool from the Attorney General of Alabama!

Money was there!

The big automobile was there!

The social life was there!

Everything was there!

BUT JESUS WASN'T THERE!

All it amounted to was that we had a lot of drunken friends! I had become so afflicted again that I couldn't even get out and drive. If I went anywhere where I was going to be up for more than an hour or two, I'd have to go to bed. Someone would have to drive me, because I'd just go to sleep. There I was, seemingly trapped and hopeless and getting ready to die, even though *I'd achieved what I'd started out to achieve many years before.*

I COULDN'T GO ON!

Deep down inside of me I still knew that there was hope in the Lord, but I didn't know how to get it. I thought it was *in me,* because of the motivational training and all the occult that we had gotten into, and the mind-idolatry-type thing.

I THOUGHT THE ANSWER WAS IN ME!

I still believed that I could think myself well. I used to go through rituals to get well. These were some of the occult formulas I had learned. "Stand before a mirror; talk to yourself in the mirror."

I used to say, "I'm healthy, I'm well; I'm healthy, I'm well; I feel great!" I would sleep on a sleep tape all night that said, "I am free from smoking." I kept on smoking. I wanted to quit, but I couldn't.

The tape would repeat, "I'm in love with my wife." It said all kinds of things. It said, "I am healthy and I am happy and I am alert and I am well." This would play over and over, going into my mind all night.

I did all the things that you're supposed to do cult-wise and became very positive in that. But, MY

CONFESSION WAS NOT RIGHT. Too many people don't understand that. My confession was, "I am well." That is not right, because the Bible says, "by his stripes I am healed." It's what Jesus did that provided healing.

I finally decided that cults weren't the answer. I didn't know what I was going to do. We tried a little Yoga and a few things like that. I thought that would get me well.

THAT DIDN'T WORK EITHER.

Since I was mostly confined to bed, I started watching the church programs on television. They were of interest to me because I knew that I had tried everything else! Actually, it was the Holy Spirit drawing us back in a way that down deep in our hearts we knew was the only way!

There was an evangelist talking on television one day. I don't even remember his name. I just remember that he was at a Baptist Church near Montgomery, Alabama. I wish I knew his name today, because if I did, I would go up and put my arms around him and thank him! Maybe I'll have to wait until I get to heaven to do that. I remember he was in his eighties and was a guest at the church.

He said, "Maybe you're not going to the church because of the hypocrites."

Boy, if there was any message that I thought needed to be preached, it was that!

I said, "That's right, because I know what those hypocrites in church are like." Then I added, "Preach on, because that's a message that needs to be preached for the hypocrites in the church."

I remember he had an old crooked finger, and he pointed it right at the TV camera, and said, "I'll tell you something about the hypocrites. At least they're trying! You ain't doing anything."

I remember that when he said that, it was just as if the Holy Spirit ran something clear through me! I REALIZED THAT I WAS NOT DOING ANYTHING ABOUT MY RELATIONSHIP TO GOD!

I told Phyllis about it. She was living in great fear, too, just as I was, because we were depending upon ourselves. The finances were shaky in the company. Even though the money was coming in, it was shaky.

We found ourselves by a bed upstairs in our room. We made an altar out of that bed, I guess. We started praying, crying out to God. We both cried and prayed. I don't remember all that happened, but I know that God really got hold of our hearts.

JESUS BECAME REAL IN OUR LIVES AGAIN AT THAT EXACT TIME!

# GOD, WE'LL DO ANYTHING!

We decided that we'd do *anything God wanted us to.* We started praying for the Lord to show us what he wanted. And he did! Shortly after that, on Easter Sunday, God spoke to our entire family. He told us to go back to Phoenix, Arizona, and work in that little church.

WE DIDN'T KNOW WHAT GOD PLANNED, BUT WE KNEW WHAT HE SAID!

He spoke to each one of us. There was a perfect harmony in what we thought.

I called the company and said, "I'm quitting my job. We're going to Phoenix. I'm going to work in the church." I told them we had already trained another man. We had trained him because I hadn't been able to work.

My boss said, "Gene, you can't quit, because you won't have any insurance. You don't have any education. You only graduated from high school, Gene, and with no education, there's no way you can quit a job like you have now, making all the money you're making. You've got to think, because the money is there."

I said, "It doesn't make any difference about the money because I'M NOT GOING TO MISS THE LORD. That's what he told me to do, and *I'm going to serve him!*"

We moved back to Phoenix. I was almost at the point of collapse by the time we got there. I went to a Christian doctor. He saw that I was extremely ill.

He tested my blood sugar, AND IT WAS 639 when it should have been between 80 and 120.

My triglycerides, which were supposed to be 90, were 2,075.

The scar tissue on my brain was hurting so badly that at night I COULDN'T EVEN LIE DOWN.

I COULDN'T EVEN KEEP MY HEAD ON THE PILLOW,

I COULDN'T EVEN COMB MY HAIR SOMETIMES.

I was on a walker. My multiple sclerosis was so bad I could hardly get around, and now I had sugar diabetes and other illnesses!

We went to church that first morning and there were just a few people present. This church was not a Charismatic church and didn't know much about healing, because healing wasn't taught.

During this time I was desperately seeking the Lord. I couldn't get out and had to spend most of my time in bed. The doctor put me on insulin and was working to get my sugar down, but it didn't work. My health was continually getting worse. I WAS GETTING CLOSER AND CLOSER TO DEATH!

I had a lot of time to commune with the Lord. I would stay in my bedroom and read the Bible. I praise God for that time. I'd read the word and pray. On Sunday night I would minister at the little church. I'd get in the walker or else I'd get in a chair in front of that small group of people and share the Bible. When I'd share the Bible with them, I would read and speak exactly the same words that Jesus or Paul, Peter or one of the other disciples did.

When Jesus or the disciples spoke, people came to Jesus, people were healed and miracles happened! I spoke the same words that they spoke, and it just seemed like they dribbled off the end of my lip! It never did anything for anybody I was speaking to. I couldn't understand it. The church wasn't growing at all. I'd invite people to come to church and they'd come one time, and that would be it.

One day in my bedroom I was troubled that what happened in the Bible wasn't happening in my ministry. I slid off the bed and made an altar right there. I was on my knees and I said, "Lord Jesus, I don't know what the power was that Peter and Paul and all those guys had that made things happen when they spoke your word, but I know one thing, WHATEVER IT WAS, I HAVEN'T GOT IT BECAUSE WHEN I SPEAK THEM, *NOTHING HAPPENS!* WHATEVER THAT POWER WAS THEY HAD I WANT YOU TO GIVE IT TO ME!"

Glory to God, *he gave it to me right then!* He baptized me with the Holy Ghost! I didn't know what it was that was happening to me. I'd never heard of speaking in tongues. I had never heard of an individual praising the Lord that way. I didn't have any idea about the gifts of the Spirit, but there was a welling up inside of me. The room filled with the glory of God and a great light seemed to illuminate the entire room. But the most thrilling thing was that Jesus was so close!

I got up, pulled myself up on my walker and went to the bathroom. That was my prayer closet. I started praising the Lord and it wasn't coming out in English! As I prayed in this new language it seemed that I was getting filled with the Lord! I HAD A HALLELUJAH TIME RIGHT THERE IN THE BATHROOM!

I couldn't tell Phyllis what happened because I knew she didn't know any more about it than I did, and I knew I couldn't explain it.

The next day I went back into the bathroom and started praising the Lord, and the same thing happened again! The presence of the Lord seemed to fill the bathroom, and as I stood there praising the Lord, something interesting started happening in my life. JESUS BECAME MORE REAL!

> *And in the same way — by our faith — the Holy Spirit helps us with our daily problems and in our praying. For we don't even know what we should pray for, nor how to pray as we should; but the Holy Spirit prays for us with such feeling that it cannot be expressed in words.* *(Romans 8:26)*

At that time I did not know how to pray as I should, and the Spirit was making intercession for me to get rid of the unbelief and the doubt in my life and open up the word to me. I developed a hunger for the word, and earnestly started reading it.

People would come to see us and we'd ask them to come to church. Lo and behold, they'd come. And you know, they'd come back again the next week! Things started happening and I knew I wasn't doing anything different.

In a short time we had fifty there. I still did not know what had happened to me, but I continued reading and praising God and speaking in tongues, even though I didn't know what it was that made me feel so good!

Some brothers in the church talked to me about their seeking the baptism of the Holy Spirit. I explained to them that about a month before, something had happened to me. It was then that I realized I had received the baptism in the Holy Spirit and what it was. IT WAS IN THE BIBLE, BUT UNTIL THEN I DIDN'T KNOW WHAT IT MEANT. Then I realized what had changed my life and why people were coming to church.

Things had gotten worse for us financially and we went to live with Phyllis' mom and dad. One Sunday morning I said, "Phyllis, let's pray for you to receive the baptism." We prayed and the Lord really blessed her. She didn't receive her prayer language at that time, but because of her yielding herself to God, she found a new love for Jesus. We went to church that day full of joy in the Lord, and the Lord appeared to Phyllis in a vision. He stretched his arms forth and said, "Come on, Phyllis. It's all right."

The Lord spoke to us to go to Orlando, Florida. I didn't know why. I had some friends there, but I didn't have any reason to go whatsoever, except I knew God had spoken to our hearts to go there. Phyllis knew, too.

I told my doctor what God had said, and the doctors started getting their heads together and said, "There's no way you can make the trip. You'll die before you can get across the country."

"Well," I said, "I might die, but I didn't go to Africa when I was twenty when God told me to and I'd rather die in Mississippi or Louisiana or somewhere trying to do what God told me to do than to miss the will of the Lord again. I'm not going to go through another fourteen years of being away from God as I did before."

They did what they could for me in order to try and get me stabilized for the trip. They didn't know it, but I had a lot bigger problem than dying. WE DIDN'T HAVE ENOUGH MONEY TO BUY THE FIRST TANKFUL OF GAS. Phyllis had been so faithful so many times when we'd gone broke. She'd have to sell the very last little bit of what she had many times in order for us to eat. So again she packed up what remaining things we had, dishes and books and I don't even know what all, and took them down to the parking lot in Phoenix and sold them. That was the money we had for gas and food to go across the country.

# "JESUS, OVERHAUL HIM!"

We finally made it to Orlando. When we got there we moved in with some friends. We didn't have any money to get a house.

Our friends were Methodists and the next Sunday we started going to church with them. They said, "We don't normally go to this church, but you know some people there and I think you might enjoy it." It was the Calvary Assembly of God. The pastor, Roy Harthern, was preaching.

I'd never seen so many people in one church in my life and I had to sit in a steel chair in an aisle. I'd gotten in there on my walker and I thought, "Man, I don't know what is going on here, but it must be good to have this many people." They were clapping their hands, praising the Lord, and were singing like I had never heard before! I don't mind telling you, I liked it! Then I started hearing the word and it said the Lord was alive! HE'S ALIVE TODAY! He's not a dead God today! HE'S ALIVE! He wants to meet your need, whatever it is!

The pastor said, "If you're sick, the Lord will heal you.

"If you're broke the Lord wants to prosper you.

"If you're lost he wants to save you."

Man, I'll tell you, almost every need he mentioned, I had. Praise God! With myself in that state I knew that I'd found a home! That was when the Lord revealed to me Jeremiah 32:27:

> Behold, I am the Lord, the God of all flesh: is there any thing too hard for me? (KJV)

I realized it wasn't too hard for God to give what he wanted for me.

I went back Wednesday night and the pastor was preaching on the word again. He was preaching on Proverbs 4:20-22.

> My son, attend to my words; incline thine ear unto my sayings. Let them not depart from thine eyes; keep them in the midst of thine heart. For they ARE life unto those that find them, and health to all their flesh. (KJV)

I wanted to jump up in the middle of that service and shout hallelujah! For the first time in my life I had been "diagnosed!" In almost nineteen years of sickness, I was diagnosed, but I was told I had multiple sclerosis, and I did have; I had scar tissue, diabetes, and a lot of other things. But my real problem, according to the word of God, was that I HAD A SHORTAGE OF THE WORD! It said that if I had the word in me and I had it in my heart, it would be life to me and it would be health to my flesh. I did not have abundant life, and I didn't have health. I HAD A SHORTAGE OF THE WORD.

Then I found out that the Lord said in Psalms 107:20,

> He sent his word, and healed them, and delivered them from their destructions. (KJV)

I kept reading and found out that it said in Psalms 103: 1-3,

> *Bless the Lord, O my soul: and all that is*
> *within me, bless his holy name. Bless the*
> *Lord, O my soul, and forget not all his*
> *benefits: Who forgiveth all thine iniquities;*
> *who healeth all thy diseases. (KJV)*

I believed that. I believed that Jesus had shed his blood for me and washed away my sins, and therefore, I WAS washed and set free from sin. But the second half of that third verse said, "who healeth all thy diseases." And I didn't even know that was in the Bible!

The Holy Spirit led me into repentance for unbelief and doubt. The thing I was repenting of was, how can I believe only half a verse? If I believed the first half, how could I not believe the second half? I really tried and it quickened in my spirit.

Then, I discovered something else. It was in Isaiah 53:5,

> *But he was wounded for our transgres-*
> *sions, he was bruised for our iniquities:*
> *the chastisement of our peace was upon*
> *him; and with his stripes we are healed.*
> *(KJV)*

Isaiah had that beautiful vision seven hundred years before Jesus ever came to earth as a man. I remember looking at the footnotes at the side of the references, and it had I Peter 2:24 and I turned in my Bible to read there. It said,

> *Who his own self bare our sins in his own*
> *body on the tree that we, being dead to*
> *sins, should live unto righteousness: by*
> *whose stripes ye were healed. (KJV)*

Peter wrote that 64 years after the cross and I knew that the "were" healed had already happened. We were saved, but I ran around lost a long time. Jesus had paid the price for my sins and I started seeing he had also paid the price for my healing.

Then I read in Matthew 8:14-15 where Jesus walked into Peter's house and saw his mother-in-law sick of a fever. She was sick, and he touched her hand and the fever left her immediately. It said that she got up and was restored whole right then. She got up and ministered to them. That evening they brought to him many who were possessed with devils and he cast out the spirits WITH HIS WORD and healed ALL that were sick. Then it said in Matthew 8:17 that this fulfilled the prophecy of Isaiah, "Himself took our infirmities, and bare our sicknesses." That said to me (the Holy Spirit made it so real) at that time, "Himself took MY infirmities." JESUS took MY infirmities and bore my sicknesses.

I started realizing when that lash cut deep into his back that my multiple sclerosis went into his body just like my sin went into him on the cross. When the whip came down and cut his back again my sugar diabetes went into him, I was made whole by the stripes on Jesus' back. Well, I started saying, "Lord, what have I got to do because I had to receive Jesus in order to receive eternal life. What do I have to do to be healed?"

In Mark 16:17-18 Jesus said,

> *"And these signs shall follow them that believe; In my name . . . they shall lay hands on the sick, and they shall recover."*

Then I saw in James 5:15 that it said,

> *And the prayer of faith shall save the sick, and the Lord shall raise him up.*

I kept meditating on these scriptures and seeing that Jesus wanted to heal me and I kept praying. I thought, "Well, I don't understand the prayer of faith." I wondered if maybe it will take somebody that has a lot of faith to pray the prayer of faith." I thought if somebody had seen people healed, then THEY would know how to pray the prayer of faith.

Someone gave me a copy of the book, SINCE JESUS PASSED BY by Charles and Frances Hunter. I read it and it really ministered to me. I thought, "Well, if the Hunters or somebody would pray for me because they've had a lot of great healings in their ministry (not because of the fact that they had healing power in them, but because of the fact that Charles and Frances had seen people healed) they would have the faith I was looking for. It would be easy for them to believe and pray the prayer of faith.

I found out that they were coming to Orlando. I KNEW THAT WAS MY NIGHT TO BE HEALED!

There were no steps in the building where I was going to be healed, so I didn't even take my walker!

Phyllis and Doug helped me out of the car and half dragged, half carried me into the building. The Holy Spirit had revealed to me that when I went to be prayed for, it would be no different than when I prayed the sinner's prayer — I would be made whole! I HAD NO DOUBT ABOUT IT! There was no reason to think the Bible was not right; it was right and meant what it said!

People were getting healed all over the place. A man just four or five seats from me was healed of a deaf ear.

Praise God!

A lot of people I knew got healed, and I thought, "Hallelujah! this is my night!!"

We stood up then and started singing and praising the Lord. When I stood I got such a severe pain in my back I didn't think I was going to be able to sit down. Here came the word from the devil. He said, "You're going to have to leave because you can't sit down." I just believed God and said, "God, you wouldn't want me out of here; even if I wasn't going to be healed, Lord, you wouldn't want me to leave here. This is too beautiful."

I did sit down, and as soon as I started to sit the pain left.

I wondered when it would happen to me. The service continued and nothing happened to me. The service ended — and still I wasn't healed.

BUT I KNEW THIS WAS MY NIGHT TO BE HEALED.

Could I have been wrong? "But Jesus, it is in your word and I believe it." They dismissed the service. Then Frances said, "If anybody has come with a need that hasn't been met, we want you to come forward. We're going to pray for you."

When Frances said that I got up out of my chair and started making my way to the front, one row at a time, hanging onto the chairs because I didn't have my walker and nobody was taking me up. I finally got up there. Frances said to me, "What's the matter with you?"

"I've got multiple sclerosis, scar tissue on my brain, sugar diabetes, a high cholesterol and I'm dying."

At that point I got the biggest surprise of my life. She looked at me and said, "Praise Jesus!"

I thought she had to be the hardest hearted woman in the world to say something like that to somebody dying. I didn't understand. Then what she prayed astounded me. She very simply, excitedly, said, "What you need is a Jesus overhaul." She placed both of her hands gently on the sides of my head and said, "JESUS, OVERHAUL HIM!"

MY FAITH IGNITED — SHE DIDN'T LIMIT GOD!

She didn't ask God to keep me from hurting. She didn't say "if it be thy will." She didn't limit God at all! She said, "Jesus, overhaul him!"

She was the first person, I believe, who ever prayed for me who DIDN'T LIMIT GOD!

I began falling backwards. I hit the floor like a ton of bricks. I fell under the power of God. I didn't know that would ever happen to me, but it certainly did.

As I lay there on the floor I remember hitting someone behind me and he went "oof" and I hit the floor. I later discovered it was the usher catching me. I had gone backwards harder than he expected.

I KNEW I HAD BEEN TOUCHED BY THE POWER OF GOD.

As I lay there on the floor it was like there was a great blinding light came before me. It felt like God had a blow torch on the scar tissue on my brain at the back of my head and it was burning. There were waves of light that went over me. Then it was like my spinal cord was a piece of rubber and someone took it and shook it and flopped it around. I don't know how long I was under the power, maybe five or ten minutes, or more. I started feeling healing.

The first thing I noticed was that my feet began to hurt! My feet had been numb for years and I couldn't tell whether my shoes fit or not, but ALL OF A SUDDEN MY SHOES BEGAN TO PINCH MY FEET! I knew something was happening because there had been absolutely no feeling there for years. PRAISE GOD, THEY WERE ACTUALLY HURTING!

Then feeling began to come into my legs! Then in my arms!! I started rubbing my arm. I could feel my hand on my arm as I lay there under the power of God. I was not unconscious — I was aware of what was going on and I KNEW A LOT WAS GOING ON!

The next thing that happened was, to me, the most exciting part of the miracle God was performing.

I STOOD UP!

The most difficult thing for an M.S. victim to do is to stand up once you are down. Your equilibrium has been lost. It's almost like you're drunk.

THERE HAD TO BE A GREAT HEALING!

I stood up!

I COULD STAND!

Then I started to walk! Praise God! I started walking back unassisted to my seat without holding on to anything or anyone! I began straightening up. Every step I took I got stronger.

I knew that because God's word is true, HE HAD HEALED ME!

# WHAT FOLLOWS HEALING?

One of the questions most often asked about healings, is, "Do they last?"

The same question can be asked about salvation, "Does it last?"

The same answer can be given to both questions, "Not if Satan can prevent it."

But God's word is true and Jesus made full and complete arrangements while he was visiting earth for our eternal salvation and health.

On Thursday night, December 13, 1973, I WAS HEALED of multiple sclerosis, sugar diabetes, scar tissue on my brain, and excessively high cholesterol and triglycerides.

I woke up the next morning, December 14, 1973, with a new experience! I got up feeling good. Glory to God! I cannot remember during nineteen years of sickness, getting up feeling good. I GOT UP WHOLE. I never knew what it was like to feel whole. I had a little spot of pain in my back, but it was like a sore muscle, nothing serious. The whole weekend was real good and so was Monday.

I wanted to get in touch with the doctor. I wanted to find out about my sugar, but he was out of town. Charles and Frances had said during the miracle service that if anyone healed was under the care of a physician or on medication prescribed, to continue the medication until the doctor examined you and let him tell you what to do.

To those who are not familiar with sugar diabetes (Diabetes Mellitus), let me explain, in language I understand, a little about it. When you have diabetes, the sugar content gets too high in your blood.

In my case, the highest measurement was 639 when it should have been between 80 and 120. This was a severe case of diabetes. The symptoms and reactions I had were weakness and nausea and I would perspire heavily. At times I would pass out (faint). My doctor had me wear a metal bracelet, on the back of which was engraved "DIABETIC." This was worn so that if I was found unconscious or helpless, I would be properly treated for diabetes. Time (in receiving treatment) is important when this condition exists. *I cut the bracelet off the night I was healed!*

Diabetics are generally taught how to test the sugar content of the blood so they can regulate the intake of sugar into their blood. A little test tape is inserted into a urine sample and the tape changes color, thus identifying excessive sugar. Insulin is the medication normally used to cause the excess sugar to be stored in such places as the liver and muscles; then the sugar is returned to the blood in small quantities. Proper dieting, rest and other care is needed for survival. Too little sugar can cause serious reactions just as well as too much, so you have to maintain a proper balance. I was instructed to drink orange juice and eat candy or other sweets to raise the sugar, and to take insulin along with a restricted diet to lower the sugar content.

When I was not able to reach my doctor the morning after I was healed, to have him examine me, I did what Charles and Frances suggested. I TOOK A PRETTY

LARGE DOSE OF INSULIN. In about two hours I started getting shaky and weak. I knew this meant I had too little sugar. IT MEANT SOMETHING HAD HAPPENED! It meant my sugar diabetes had been healed — IT WAS GONE! I was excited because this was the first identifiable evidence I had seen of this part of my healing. MY FAITH IGNITED AGAIN! To counteract the effect of the insulin, I started drinking orange juice and eating candy bars, and still felt most of the day like I was going into insulin shock because the sugar was gone out of my blood stream. Praise God, IT WAS GONE!

When my doctor got back, I told him I had been healed. He wanted to know who healed me, and I said, "Jesus!"

"Jesus who?" he snapped. He assured me that the Lord couldn't do anything for me and that I was just going to die.

That was when a battle began within me. Satan really got in the door by putting doubt in my mind. God had been so complete in teaching me what his word said about healing. I BELIEVED IT! Then he healed me and gave me positive evidences of my healings.

I would periodically check my urine and the test would at times be positive, showing it contained sugar. I would rebuke it, SPEAK THE WORD, and in ten or fifteen minutes test it again and there would be no sugar! It just doesn't work that way. You either have it, or you don't have it!

It was a demonic presence. I never took any medication for any of the illnesses after that one insulin shot the morning after I was healed. It was interesting to me because at the time of each attack, I had a chance either to pray and battle the devil or accept the sickness. "Submit yourself therefore to God. Resist the devil, and he will flee from you." (James 4:7 KJV)

I had a choice each time to confess this powerful promise of God — a choice of submitting myself to God and resisting the devil — or of submitting to the devil and his symptoms and resisting God. Praise God, he had made my belief in his word so solid that Satan could not shake it. That's why Jesus said it was so important to study the word and hide it in our hearts. An hour or more each day meditating in the Bible and talking to God is more vital than I thought my life-giving insulin was. I could have died without the insulin, but even more real, I could have died without the word! IT KEPT ME ALIVE WITH EACH ATTACK!

I was sure of my healings. They were just like the word said. But the negative power of Satan is strong — and simple, but very deceiving. He put "doubt" into my mind; it became so strong at times that I was tempted to listen to him. I almost believed him! "Almost thou persuadeth me to be sick."

My life had been directed around sickness for that whole nineteen years, and around my infirmities. My mind had been filled with belief in sickness. The devil is not going to let go of his teachings easily. He wants you to believe, knowing that if you believe him you will succeed in accepting his inflicted physical, mental and spiritual sicknesses. Believe me, Satan is going to always put up a battle when God is doing a work. My life had revolved around something that belonged to the devil, so he wasn't going to let something happen that would give credit to God, if he could prevent it!

But God's army is ready to do battle against Satan if we will believe in God and listen to his voice. God will always win if we will do our part. He even wins by allowing us to go through trials, difficulties and problems. He makes our faith stronger. He never allows these tests to come just to see if we can fail. He wants us to win, because when we do, it's easier to have faith to believe in him once we have won the battle. He allowed me to be severely tried, but I learned to distinguish the silent, soft voice of his Holy Spirit from the boisterous, enticing, deceiving voice of Satan.

The symptoms of "his" diseases (I used to call them "mine") came back time after time. I had been asked to give my testimony at church on Wednesday night a week after my healing. Just before I was to speak, I broke out in a heavy sweat exactly like I always did when my sugar was too high. I almost soaked my clothes in the pew. As I sat there, I got so weak I thought I wasn't going to be able to get up. But I rebuked those thoughts and in my mind I kept thinking, "I'm not going to receive this because the Lord healed me, and I KNOW HE HEALED ME because the sugar is gone from my bloodstream. The diabetes is gone, and so I'm not going to accept it and I am going to testify to the church of my healing.

*As soon as I got up to testify, all the symptoms left!*

I had heard the very apparent voice of Satan say, by the symptoms and accompanying thoughts of fear, that I wasn't healed. Doubt came because of the symptoms. But the word of God had taught me that fear, doubt and sickness all come from the devil. I had received the word of God in my mind and heart and believed what it said. All the scriptures I mentioned to you earlier were a part of my inner belief and memory. They were my source of stability and I let them become my thoughts at the time of the symptoms.

I had recorded Psalms 118:17 in my mind and it was available to my memory with each attack of the devil, "I shall not die, but live, and declare the works of the Lord." I boldly, quickly and frequently declared the healing of the Lord to everyone I could, but perhaps of more importance, I declared it to myself — in my own mind as thoughts.

When I depended on mind-control tactics to battle diseases, I declared to a mirror, "I am well, I am well, I am well." But I didn't declare the works of the Lord. I was now able to testify boldly that it was the Lord who did it. Where I once confessed my infirmities, I now confessed his word, "By his stripes, I AM healed."

I could feel the presence of the Holy Spirit when I was in the church. It was there that God had first removed the symptoms as I stood to declare the works of the Lord. The church daily became my intensive care room and my recovery room during this recovery period. I needed a place sterilized by the cleansing power of the Holy Spirit, to be away from the polluted atmosphere of Satan's deceiving symptoms and lies. Almost every day for the next four or five weeks I went to the church, knelt at the altar alone and talked to God for ten to fifteen minutes. Most of the time, nobody knew this.

You have probably seen cartoons of a dog chasing a cat as fast as they could run, and suddenly the cat jumped behind a tree and took a deep breath or two, then the chase began again. That's the way I felt. I would go to the church, take a deep breath of the presence of God, and then return home.

I asked others to pray with me when the battle got rough. It got so bad at times after the first week, that I spent the biggest part of that five weeks in the word, in prayer, and testifying about my healing.

I would, at times, get numbness over my whole body. It would come like waves over my body and then I would rebuke it and say, "I won't receive this; by his stripes I am healed AND I KNOW I'M HEALED. Because I have been healed, I won't accept it back." Right away feeling came back as the numbness left. The numbness would not go immediately, but gradually would go away while I was saying to it, "I won't receive this; by his stripes I AM HEALED."

There were times when the devil attacked me with this numbness and other symptoms that we met in full battle in the bathroom. I don't mind telling you I really got to shouting the WORD at him a few times because, you know, he has a little problem with his hearing. I know there is nothing in volume. It is the authority of

Jesus by which the devil is defeated, but it helps *me* when I use a little volume!

These symptoms were just as real to me as the actual diseases. I believe I had every symptom of every illness with which I had previously been afflicted. The pain of the scar tissue on my brain returned as intense as before. It used to be so strong that I would black out. It was somewhat like somebody thrust a knife right down through my skull into my brain where the scar tissue was growing. The pain shot into my brain. The scar tissue was a growth on my brain which became inflamed at times. It's like a swelling condition of the brain. As it grows, it causes this intense pain. The pain that came after I was healed felt just a little different, but it appeared the same. I learned to identify the difference in the feeling. I learned to quickly recognize the voice of Satan. I knew the difference between the way Jesus spoke and the way Satan spoke. I learned after my healing that the devil and all his helpers talked to me just as real as when I talk to Phyllis, Doug or Gina. As soon as I had this pain, here would come a whole flood of doubt and fear into my mind, just as plain as if they were saying, "You know you're not really healed."

The whole five weeks was a battle of, "Am I going to believe what God said he had done, or am I going to believe all this other gossip that is coming into my head?" I constantly prayed, praised God and testified of the healing.

These attacks went from very severe the first week to less and less and less until at the end of five weeks there was hardly any trouble. It seemed like the devil let go gradually, or else the word became so much more real to me, and the victory became so much more real that I didn't hear what he was saying.

Even after more than two years have passed, once in a great while I'll have a short visit from the devil. Recently, a wave of numbness flowed over my body and the devil said, "See, you're getting sick again; your healing of M.S. was just a remission." I prayed, rebuked it in Jesus' name, and went on about my business for Jesus, and it left right away. If a symptom of stiffness or something else related to the signs of M.S., or a thought about it comes into my mind, I quote the word, "I shall not die, but live, and declare the works of the Lord." I go right on with what I am doing at the time and have no more trouble.

Another portion of scripture that has been important to me when these thoughts come into my mind, is II Corinthians 10:3-5:

> For though we walk in the flesh, we do not war after the flesh: (For the weapons of our warfare are not carnal, but mighty through God to the pulling down of strong holds;) Casting down imaginations, and every high thing that exalteth itself against the knowledge of God, and bringing into captivity every thought to the obedience of Christ; (KJV)

The attacks by *thought* have been as severe as the attack by symptoms of illness, but by the word of God and the power of the Holy Spirit, I have brought into captivity every thought to the obedience of Christ. Every thought the devil has put into my mind has been replaced with what the word of God says.

The prayers, the word, the fellowship with those who believe in healing, the praises to God and the confessing of the healing, giving the glory to God, are so important.

I believe if a person is healed, he should do everything possible to be around believers, especially during the early period following the healing. He should be in church where healings frequently occur so he will be in an atmosphere of belief. My friends and my church stood close by me during my first trying five weeks. Sometimes a family will not even believe when the evidence of healing is present. Little do they realize that their unbelief may cause their loved one to return to suffering and death. Jesus saw unbelief at work when he returned to his home town. He only did a few miracles because of their unbelief.

When a person gives his life to Jesus and is born again, his priorities change. He can go on, like I chose to do, and serve Jesus, or he can return to his old ways of sinning, like I did so many years. Priorities of desires, activities, habits and environment must change or the devil will come to steal and kill. He wants to defeat our healing the same way. But Jesus is the winner if we do our part!

The night I went to the Hunter meeting, I KNEW BEFORE I WENT THAT WHEN I WAS PRAYED FOR, I WAS GOING TO BE HEALED. I ALSO KNEW THAT IT WOULDN'T BE ANY DIFFERENT FIVE WEEKS LATER, BECAUSE I KNEW THAT WAS WHAT THE LORD HAD FOR ME.

I had read it in his word, and I believed. I still believe, and always will, because

> **"I SHALL NOT DIE, BUT LIVE, AND DECLARE THE WORKS OF THE LORD."**

Jesus certainly won in my body! My health is better than most people. I feel good continually. My strength is with me from the time I wake up until I end long days of work, ministering and traveling. I have been given a supernatural energy by the Lord that never seems to have an end. I recently walked miles in Grand Cayman as we ministered in rural areas. There is no pain in my head from the scar tissue.

I praise God for the mighty miracle of salvation and transformation of my spiritual life and for the power of the Holy Spirit given. I praise him for doing the same for Phyllis. I praise him will all my heart and give him all the glory that I have been totally healed of sugar diabetes, multiple sclerosis, scar tissue on my brain, high cholesterol, and high triglycerides — I shout praises that he gave me a total, complete and lasting JESUS OVERHAUL!

A copy of a letter from my Chrisitan doctor is reprinted here so you can rejoice with me in the mighty acts of God — all in the name of JESUS!

E. RANDALL HORTON, D.O.
Osteopathic Physician
3614 Webber Street
Sarasota, Florida 33580
Phone 921 6691

November 27, 1974

TO WHOM IT MAY CONCERN:

This is to state that Mr. Gene Lilly was first seen and
examined by me on June 1, 1973. As a result of our exam-
ination and history, we confirmed that he was suffering
from multiple sclerosis and that he also had diabetes
mellitus.

A urinalysis performed in our office June 1, 1973 showed a
4 plus sugar and a 2 plus acetone. Subsequent laboratory
tests confirmed the diabetes and he was then referred to
an internist. Copies of letters and reports concerning
Mr. Lilly's condition are attached herewith. We last
saw Mr. Lilly on August 15, 1973 at which time he was
still being treated for the diabetes and multiple sclerosis.

We did not see Mr. Lilly again until April 1, 1974. Exam-
ination then revealed no signs or symptoms of multiple
sclerosis or diabetes and a blood sugar determination
showed his blood sugar to be in normal range. He was
able to walk unassisted and even could run as he demon-
strated to us. It is our clinical impression that he has
been completely cured both of his diabetes and multiple
sclerosis.

*E. Randall Horton, D.O.*

E. Randall Horton, D. O.

ERH:mj

Roy A Harthern, Gene's pastor says:

"This is the story of a miracle of healing, but even more important than the actual healing is the way the author discovered the source of faith to bring the power of God into his own life to meet his personal needs.

"When I first met Gene, he was writing a book to encourage sick people to 'rejoice in their sufferings.' That book was never published because Gene found the source of healing and God has not only healed him, but has also given him a ministry of building faith through the Word of God and many people are being healed through his ministry. Gene began to meditate on the truth of healing and he confessed the Word of God every day until it influenced his thinking and changed his believing.

"I knew Gene Lilly when he could not walk without the aid of a 'walker.' He suffered from multiple sclerosis, sugar diabetes and other complications. Physically he was a pathetic sight.

"I know Gene Lilly today. It has been over two years since his healing, and his experience is a testimony that God still heals today."

# FREELY GIVE . . .

*by Charles*

*And as ye go, preach, saying, The king-
dom of heaven is at hand. Heal the sick,
cleanse the lepers, raise the dead, cast out
devils: freely ye have received, freely give.
(Matthew 10:7-8 KJV)*

A very vital part of Gene's maintenance of his healing
was by his testimony to everyone who would listen, telling them that God had healed him.

He told them what the Bible said!

He ministered at every opportunity to others!

He even made opportunities by his bubbling joy and
excitement about the wonders of his new life in Jesus.

He led many to Jesus. Many Christians found power
in their life as he ministered the baptism of the Holy
Spirit. At every opportunity, he prayed for the sick and
healings began to happen more and more frequently. The
more healings and deliverances that occurred, the more
God opened doors to him.

Gene had freely received — abundantly, and he un-
selfishly gave to others with all his heart and new-found
strength.

Here are some excerpts from a letter from Gene telling how God is using him.

"Sally S. had pain in her breast for several months. Her mother had died with cancer. Sally was very frightened. She went to the doctor on Monday and he confirmed that there were suspicious lumps and that she would have to enter the hospital on Friday for further tests. On Wednesday Phyllis and I prayed for her. Friday she entered the hospital where they made tests and took X-rays. She just KNEW it was so bad they could do nothing about it. In came the radiologist, and said, 'Why did your doctor put you in the hospital? What did he think you had? We can find NOTHING.'

"Evelyn D. writes: 'For several years, I had suffered every day and night with agonizing sharp pains from arthritis and arthritic spurs in the vertebrae of my spine. This necessitated my sleeping with a cervical collar on a special pillow. I was able to get very little rest or sleep and was always tired, tense and nervous and rather irritable at times. Quite often I wore the cervical collar during the day at home and in the office. In addition to the surgical traction device that I used at home, I went for physical therapy and traction as an out-patient at a local hospital. I gave this up as it was expensive and the treatments only gave me temporary relief. On several occasions I even tried to get relief with alcohol. At times the arthritis affected the use of my hands and fingers. The numbness in my hands caused me to drop things in the kitchen and the office. I found I could not type or hold a pencil on some of my bad days. The tension and lack of rest caused me in addition to suffer with tension or migraine headaches almost constantly.

"'On September 11, 1975, Gene Lilly prayed for me. Since my healing, I have discontinued the use of the surgical collar and traction device. I have discontinued the use of aspirin and all medication. I feel ten years younger and my family tells me I am a different person. I give all glory to God. On Nov. 24, 1975, my healing was confirmed by the doctor when I was examined and X-rayed.'

"In September, 1975, Norva Lee R. was healed of bowed legs and gastritis. She has not taken any medicine since she received her healing.

"In 1974, Millie H. came to a Catholic prayer group where I was speaking. She had a tumor on her foot for which she was supposed to have surgery. The doctors had decided against it because it was on a tendon and there was a danger that it might cripple her. Millie was IN-STANTLY healed, she received the baptism of the Holy Spirit and while slain in the Spirit, the Lord Jesus Christ healed her back. She was born with a spinal curvature due to two extra discs. The spinal problem caused much discomfort in the legs. She wore a quarter-inch lift in her shoe at times. Since the healing she has not worn the lift and has been free from pain.

"April 16, 1976, Art C. came to a prayer group. He was not a Christian, had never seen anyone slain in the Spirit and came because his wife asked him to. As we prayed for Art, he fell face forward under the power and God operated on his back. When he got up he said for the first time since 1965 he had absolutely no pain in his back. He was operated on in 1965 for a ruptured disc, again in 1970 for a nerve fusion, and in 1975 for a double spinal fusion. Art was saved four days later and received the baptism of the Holy Spirit the following week. This Methodist man was healed at our prayer group, saved at a Catholic prayer group and received the baptism in an Assembly of God Church. God is good!

"In November 1975, I went to Cayman Islands, B.W.I. We ministered in a Church of Christ where a Catholic couple attended. Paula and Jerry had been married for over 30 years. They had not told each other they loved the other one for 28 years. God healed that marriage, and gave them a burning desire to work for him. They had not lived as man and wife for 8 years. God restored their love for one another.

"Tom B. came to our prayer group in January of 1976. He was 82 years old, had cataracts on both eyes, was scheduled for surgery in February. He had been a Baptist all his life and never knew anything about healing. I prayed for him on Friday night for one eye. He came back the next week and said, 'God did a good job on this left eye; now pray for the right one.' When he went to the doctor to be scheduled for the surgery, the cataracts were gone. The doctor was amazed! Praise God!"

# FAITH COMETH BY HEARING

*by Charles*

Gene has shared his testimony of the mighty power of God in his salvation and healing. Both *salvation* and *healing* were accomplished by faith. FAITH IS SIMPLY TRUSTING GOD! Lack of faith is simply not believing God. Gene finally wanted God, sought him, found him, accepted him, believed him and loved him.

It took a long time for this to happen, but all the way from a childhood conversion, through years of rebellion and sin, Gene some way, behind all the struggles, maintained a very thin thread of faith in God.

Faith to him wasn't *serving God* or else he would not have kept his faith to believe God while he wasn't serving him. Faith wasn't a mind accomplishment, or he could have thought his health back.

Faith to be saved came when God SPOKE to him. It was when God SPOKE through the voice of an eighty year old man on TV and when God used the crooked finger of this old evangelist to point at Gene, that he HEARD God SPEAK!

But HE HEARD GOD!

> **So then faith cometh by hearing, and hearing by the word of God. (Romans 10:17 KJV)**

He heard him as plainly as Moses HEARD God SPEAK from a burning bush. Having HEARD God, Moses began the work God called him years before to do. Gene and Phyllis responded to God when they cried out to him and yielded their hearts to his call. They obeyed God!

They HEARD God again a short time later on Easter Sunday when he SPOKE to the whole family to "GO!" They didn't wait. Immediate preparations were made to go to Phoenix where God SAID to go. That wasn't easy for a crippled, penniless man to take his family across the nation, not even knowing why God wanted him to go.

THAT IS FAITH!

> *By FAITH Abraham, when he was called to go out into a place which he should after receive for an inheritance, OBEYED; and he went out, not knowing whither he went. (Heb. 11:8 KJV)*

THAT IS FAITH!

That wasn't easy, either but it was what God said to do. When he obeyed, God abundantly blessed, just as he did Gene.

Did you notice how Abraham and Gene got their faith?

GOD SPOKE!
THEY HEARD!
THEY OBEYED!
THAT'S FAITH!

> **So then faith cometh by HEARING, and hearing by the word of God. (Rom 10:17 KJV)**

What is the word of God?
IT'S WHEN GOD SPEAKS!

God knows every language there is and creates multitudes of new languages. He speaks each one fluently. God speaks to ALL who will listen. Every word he speaks is exact and plain. He has a purpose when he speaks. He also knows who will listen and when. He speaks in many different ways.

> Long ago God SPOKE in many different ways to our fathers through the prophets (in visions, dreams, and even face to face), telling them little by little about his plans.
>
> But now in these days he has SPOKEN to us through his Son to whom he has given everything, and through whom he made the world and everything there is. (Hebrews 1:1-2)
>
> Then God SAID, "Let there be light." (Gen. 1:3)

What did God do? He SPOKE! What happened? Light appeared. Even light obeyed and came into being!

One day a young woman came to a morning teaching session. As she walked in, she came to me and said, "I came because I believe I will be healed when you pray." Why did she come? God, by his mighty Holy Spirit, SPOKE to her. She probably didn't think about God actually telling her to come so he could heal her. Paul remarked that he was utterly compelled by the Spirit to go . . . God SPOKE.

This young woman explained that two years before she had been in an accident which left her body crooked. Her neck was tilted, one shoulder was higher than the other, one arm shorter, her hips were uneven and one leg was shorter than the other. When she came to me for prayer, she came BELIEVING she would be healed, even though, if I remember correctly, *she had never seen anyone healed before!* I don't even know if she had read the Bible. She had HEARD that people were healed in our services, so she came to be healed.

As I stepped in front of her to pray, God SPOKE to me. He said, "Stand back, point at her body and COMMAND it to straighten!"

She had HEARD God SAY to come.

She had obeyed him.

She believed, because he SPOKE!

**So then faith cometh by HEARING, and HEARING by the word of God.**

God SPOKE to me, instructing me how to pray.

After all, Jesus spoke with authority.

*And he arose, and REBUKED the wind, and said unto the sea, Peace, be still. And the wind ceased, and there was a great calm. (Mark 4:39 KJV)*

Jesus again SPOKE when he went to Peter's house where Peter's wife's mother had a great fever.

*And he stood over her, and REBUKED the fever; and it left her; and immediately she arose and ministered unto them. (Luke 4:39 KJV)*

God told me to SPEAK to this young woman's body. God had, by his Spirit, SPOKEN to me while I was reading his written WORD about three years before. He "impressed on my mind," SPOKE to me, by letting me be aware that Jesus SPOKE to the fever. I had never thought about speaking to a disease or part of a body before that. He had SPOKEN in his WORD another time in Mark 16:17:

*And those who believe shall use my AUTHORITY to cast out demons . . . . . . and they will be able to place their hands on the sick and heal them.*

He gave me AUTHORITY to heal and deliver. How did I know? I meditated on his WORD and he SPOKE to me. Jesus said I could use his authority. I HEARD him SAY that to me in his WORD. I believed it. Now, all I had to do was put it into action.

WOULD IT WORK?

So then faith cometh by HEARING, and hearing by the word of God.

I HEARD him speak.

I HEARD it by the WORD of God.

My faith was established.

I backed away from the young woman, pointed my finger at her body, spoke to the body with the authority of Jesus, and said,

"Body, I command you in the name of Jesus, straighten!"

Immediately her neck straightened, her shoulders leveled, her hips leveled, her arms and legs became even and she almost shouted, "What's happening to me?" She had received what she came for.

She HEARD God.

She OBEYED.

She BELIEVED.

She RECEIVED!

So often we seek "FAITH."

I have sought faith for years to attempt to attain results in healing. One time, after searching and seeking over a thousand hours in the New Testament for "faith without a doubt," Jesus simply SAID to me, "Have faith in ME; not the healing." That made it so easy to have faith. Just believe in Jesus. Just believe what he SAID in the WORD. It's so simple. We try to make it so complicated.

We have discovered that when God SPEAKS to us and tells us to do something, we have ALL the faith we need. We simply do what he says. He is the giver of faith. Surely he wouldn't tell us to do something we couldn't do. Not our God!

We have learned to be sensitive *to what God says* and then with no further attempt to try for faith, we just obey.

TRUST AND OBEY
FOR THERE'S NO OTHER WAY
TO BE HAPPY IN JESUS,
BUT TO TRUST AND OBEY

Simple, isn't it?

*So then faith cometh by HEARING, and HEARING by the word of God.*

*Listen!*
*Learn his word!*
*Obey!*
*Receive!*

Be sensitive to what God *wants* you to do. Then do it!

Faith? You don't need any more than that! That's God's faith!

How did Gene receive his healings? God got his attention, saved him, and taught him a few simple, choice promises about healing. But what caused him to have faith for these remarkable healings? GOD SPOKE and GENE HEARD!

The Holy Spirit utterly compelled him to go to a church where God's Spirit was present. Gene thought his Methodist friends got misdirected. But God SPOKE by an act to bring him to a source of knowledge.

God opened Gene's ears to hear the WORD of the Lord. Gene WANTED to hear. Gene HEARD God SPEAK through a minister. Gene BELIEVED what he HEARD. He actually didn't question or doubt what God said. No doubt, he had read these words before. Maybe even heard sermons about healing and faith. But he had never HEARD God SPEAK to him. The Spirit of God had SPOKEN to the spirit of Gene — to his heart — to his understanding, receptive inner being.

GENE HEARD GOD SPEAK!

HE HEARD GOD "SPEAK" HIS WRITTEN WORD. He didn't read words in the Bible. He HEARD GOD! He believed in his heart. He knew he HEARD the word. But still he couldn't get healed by trying to apply the word.

Gene kept searching. He was sincere. He meditated on the word. He loved God. He wanted to please him.

GENE WANTED TO PLEASE GOD!

God put a thought into Gene's mind, "If somebody had seen people healed, then THEY would know how to pray the prayer of faith." Would you believe it. In effect, Gene had asked God how to get faith and God answered by SPEAKING a thought into his mind. Gene listened. He heard! God sent him a copy of SINCE JESUS PASSED BY. He read it. God SPOKE to him by showing him just what he asked; someone who had seen people healed. He wasn't seeking faith. He was searching for the way to apply the faith he already had been given. Then God sent us to Gene's hometown and let him know about it.

Immediately he KNEW he would be healed that night. He not only came — he left his walker at home.

What had happened?

GOD SPOKE!

GENE HEARD HIM SPEAK IN THE WORD!

GENE HEARD GOD SPEAK SEVERAL OTHER WAYS!

GENE BELIEVED!

HE OBEYED!

HE RECEIVED!

> So then faith cometh by hearing, and
> hearing by the word of God.

Have you a mountain to move? Are you saved? Have you been born again? Have you received the Holy Ghost since you believed? Are you sick? Are you afflicted? Do you have problems you can't solve? Do you have an evil spirit oppressing you? Do you have an attitude that controls you?

ARE YOU READY TO MOVE YOUR MOUNTAIN RIGHT NOW?

You have every ingredient you need, right now, right where you are to have your need met. You have HEARD God speak to you in the pages of this book. He has SPOKEN to you from the declaration of his WORD in this book. You believe God has spoken to you in many ways while you read this book and the scriptures.

Since you have HEARD God speak, by his word, then you already have all the faith you need!

We are going to pray with and for you right now, so be ready to "RISE AND BE HEALED!"

First, let's be sure you are a child of God.

**So then, faith cometh by hearing, and hearing by the word of God.**

Let's start by HEARING the WORD of God:

*After dark one night a Jewish religious leader named Nicodemus, a member of the sect of the Pharisees, came for an interview with Jesus. "Sir," he said, "we all know that God has sent you to teach us. Your miracles are proof enough of this."*

*Jesus replied, "With all the earnestness I possess I tell you this: Unless you are born again, you can never get into the Kingdom of God."*

*"Born again!" exclaimed Nicodemus. "What do you mean? How can an old man go back into his mother's womb and be born again?"*

*Jesus replied, "What I am telling you so earnestly is this: Unless one is born of water and the Spirit, he cannot enter the Kingdom of God. Men can only reproduce human life, but the Holy Spirit gives new life from heaven; so don't be surprised at my statement that you must be born again! (John 3:1-7)*

How do you get born again to receive this new life from heaven? Simply pray this prayer sincerely and Jesus will come into your life and save you — RIGHT NOW!

Dear Lord Jesus,
I need you to be my Savior. Forgive all of my sins. Wash me and cleanse me of all unrighteousness. Come into my life. Thank you, Jesus. Thank you for coming into my life as my Savior and Lord. I love you, Lord Jesus. Amen.

Confess right now, "I have been born again. I have new life from heaven. Jesus is my Savior and Lord."

Welcome into God's Royal Family. You are a child of God. Look up right now, smile at God, and say to him, "Father, my Father, I love you!"

Let's pray next for you if you have an attitude that you and God are not pleased with. Let's read a few verses from the Living Bible. NOW HEAR THE WORD, remembering,

*So then faith cometh by hearing, and hearing by the word of God.*

*. . . forgive us our sins, just as we have forgiven those who have sinned against us. (Matt 6:12)*

Is there anyone who has done something to you — hurt you, lied about you, cheated you, hated you, stolen a person or property from you, gossiped about you? Are you holding a grudge against anyone? Remember Jesus wants to forgive YOU, NOW. It's probably not your fault that they sinned against you. But that's not what Jesus is SAYING (SPEAKING) TO YOU — HEAR HIM — He is wanting to forgive you of *your* attitude, your reaction to their sin. You are not responsible for *their* sins — only *yours*!

Let's pray.

Father, I have been sinned against by
_____, (say the names).

My attitude has been unforgiving to them.
People sinned against Jesus and he forgave
them and wants us to be like him. So,
Father, please forgive me now just as I
forgave _____. Thank
you, Father!

**Have ye received the Holy Ghost since ye
believed? (Acts 19:2 KJV)**

**So then faith cometh by hearing, and
hearing by the word of God.**

So let's again HEAR the WORD of God.

*For John truly baptized with water; but
ye shall be baptized with the Holy Ghost
not many days hence. (Acts 1:5 KJV)*

Jesus is the baptizer with the Holy Spirit and he commands us to receive. If he commands it, he also provides
it and provides faith for it.

*And when the day of Pentecost was fully
come, they were all with one accord in
one place.*

*And suddenly there came a sound from
heaven like a rushing mighty wind, and it
filled all the house where they were sit-
ting.*

*And there appeared unto them cloven
tongues like as of fire, and it sat upon
each of them.*

*And they were all filled with the Holy
Ghost, and began to speak with other
tongues, as the Spirit gave them utterance.
(Acts 2:1-4 KJV)*

Now we have HEARD God speak through Jesus, the
WORD, and from the written word of God, so faith is
already sufficient for you to receive right now, so let's
pray:

Jesus, I believe the power you promised is available to
me right now, just like you gave on the day of Pentecost,

so I ask you, Jesus, to baptize me with the Holy Spirit. On the day of Pentecost when THEY (the 120 people) received, they ALL began praising God, and speaking in other tongues, as the Spirit gave them utterance. I know that all languages are made up of a lot of mixed up syllables and I know I can only speak one language at a time. Now, Father, I don't know a Spirit language, so I ask you to give me a new language with which to praise you, just like you did your other disciples in the Bible. I can make syllables, so I am going to do that right now as your Holy Spirit fills me and gives me the utterance.

Begin RIGHT NOW, by *faith*, praising God. Turn your heart towards God, and begin praising God, but not in English! Glory!

NOW LET'S PRAY FOR YOUR PHYSICAL HEALING, SO GET READY! After spending so much time in the word of God writing this book, and reading Gene's exciting story of faith and healing, we have enough faith right now to move your mountain of sickness or affliction.

Remember, you are qualified to be healed RIGHT NOW, and God wants to heal you, just as easy as he healed Gene.

**So then faith cometh by hearing, and hearing by the word of God.**

Your faith has already been given you so you don't need any more. You have exactly the right amount to be healed. It doesn't make any difference to God and Jesus how little or how big your mountain is. God loves to heal his children of all sizes of illnesses.

Just one more scripture before you get healed:

*And a certain man lame from his mother's womb was carried, whom they laid daily at the gate of the temple which is called Beautiful, to ask alms of them that entered into the temple:*

> *Who seeing Peter and John about to go into the temple asked an alms.*
>
> *And Peter, fastening his eyes upon him with John, said, Look on us.*
>
> *And he gave heed unto them, expecting to receive something of them.*
>
> *Then Peter said, Silver and gold have I none; but such as I have give I thee: In the name of Jesus Christ of Nazareth rise up and walk. (Acts 3:2-6 KJV)*

You have believed!

You have been given faith!

You have heard God speak!

You have heard his word . . . . .

Now Satan, you have sent some spirits causing incurable diseases of deafness, blindness, dumbness, multiple sclerosis, diabetes, arthritis, epilepsy, and many others. I speak the word to you:

Satan, we bind you by the power of the Holy Spirit. Now you spirits causing these afflictions we command you, in Jesus' name, COME OUT!

Jesus, we ask you to now heal the damage done to these bodies.

Father, we ask you now to heal any other need in the bodies, minds or souls of your child who has read this book and received your faith by hearing you speak — IN JESUS' MIGHTY NAME!

Right now,

IN THE NAME OF JESUS CHRIST OF NAZARETH, RISE UP AND WALK!

If you are lame — get up right now, in the name of Jesus — and WALK!

If you have an arm, leg, back, neck, knee or any other movable part, MOVE IT right now, in the name of Jesus!

Whatever your illness or affliction is, if you can test it, do it right now, IN THE NAME OF JESUS!

In Jesus' name, we take authority over your body and command you, body, be healed — right now!

# RISE AND BE HEALED

## IN THE NAME OF JESUS

Thank you, Father!
Thank you, Jesus!
We give you ALL the glory!

Gene and Phyllis are in full-time evangelism and travel all over the nation and into foreign countries and islands. God is mightily using them. They may be contacted at:

Love of Jesus Ministries
P.O. Box 1118
Richmond, In. 47374